# UNLOCKING YOUR PURPOSE

Keys to discovering your
God-given purpose in life

Published 2019 by Terry J Boyle
© Terry John Boyle 2019.

Unless otherwise noted, all scripture quotations are taken from the Holy Bible, New King James Version  Copyright C 1979, 1980, 1982 by Thomas Nelson, Inc.

All rights reserved. No part of this book may be reproduced in any form, stored in a retrieval system, or transmitted in any form by any means—electronic, mechanical, photocopy, recording or otherwise—without the prior written permission of the publisher, except as provided by Australian copyright law.

Words in capitals, or in bold or italics are the emphases of the author Terry Boyle – terryjohnboyle@bigpond.com

Cover & typeset by Carl Butel at Deep Image – carl@deepimage.net.au

Cataloguing-in-Publication data is available from the
National Library of Australia
ISBN 978-0-646-99846-6
eBook ISBN 978-0-646-99878-7

# Acknowledgments

For the wonderful love and support of my wife Caroline, and our children Amanda, Felicity, Andrew, Sharon, and their Spouses and Children.

To our daughter Amanda Butel for her insight, and hours of typing, also her husband Carl for the brilliant cover design and internal layout, getting this book ready to publish.

To many fellow ministers and mentors over the years. Hal Oxley for his leadership principles that he imparted to me when I was his assistant minister in Melbourne. To the late Trevor Chandler and the Brisbane Church who supported us while we were on the mission field. To John Pasterkamp together with National Leaders who invited us to start a Bible College in the city of Port Moresby, Papua New Guinea.

To all those in Lismore NSW at CLC (now Centre Church) where I served as senior pastor and chairman of the board of Summerland Christian College for 21 years. I handed over to Rod and Margaret Dymock my associates at the time. Their leadership has now taken the Church and College on to a higher level of excellence.

We are now semi-retired and reside on the Gold Coast, where we enjoy fellowshipping with several churches. We are officially affiliated with A2A.

# CONTENTS

Foreword 7
Introduction 9

**Section One**
**Opening up your Heart**
1. Living with Shark Hunters 13
2. Hidden Purposes within you 19
3. Is your heart in it? 27
4. Avoid living without a Purpose 35

**Section Two**
**Opening up your Gifting**
1. Grace for your Purpose 43
2. Discovering your Gifting 51
3. Faith to Pursue your Purpose 57
4. Inspired by Good Leaders 65

**Section Three**
**Opening up your Ministry**
1. Spreading the Gospel of the Kingdom 77
2. Helping to Plant and Establish Churches 85
3. Considering the Culture 95
4. A Home Base and Spiritual Warfare 103
5. The Purpose of Provision and Prosperity 115

**Section Four**
**Opening up your Future**
1. What does the Future look like? 122
2. Understanding Times and Seasons 131
3. Pressing on with Purpose 137

**UNLOCKING** Your **PURPOSE**

# Foreword

by Dr Allan Meyer

I first met Terry Boyle at a meeting at Life Ministry Centre where he was one of the Pastors. The Charismatic Movement was touching churches all over the nation. Life Ministry Centre under the leadership of Pastor Hal Oxley was one place a person could go to encounter that move of God. I was a High School Teacher in my early twenties with a call of God on my life. This was a critical season of life and Pastor Terry Boyle was one of those who played a critical role as an example and encourager in unlocking the purpose of my life in those formative years.

About this time Terry led my brother Neil to the Lord and played a key role in unlocking the purpose of his life. Inspired by the character and vitality of the ministry team I left my role as a teacher, took my wife and young family to LMC Bible College and later that year was appointed their first Youth Pastor.

In that first year of my ministry appointment, Terry was a friend and a coach. I was inspired and strengthened by his faith and his kindness as he prayed and ministered to people. I had hoped to acquire a perfectly positioned property in the local shopping centre as an outreach centre for our Youth Ministry, but the owner had rejected our application and rented the property to a dentist. I was deeply disappointed. Terry came to me one morning and said "God spoke to me this morning about you. He said, Tell Allan Meyer to try again". The owner reversed his decision, rented the property to us, and promptly died ten days later. That word from Terry Boyle unlocked the purpose of our youth ministry for the next three years.

Terry is the real thing – a man of God with many years of profound experience in fulfilling the call of God in his own life. He is faithful and true. I would encourage everyone to read this valuable insight to his journey through life with Jesus, but I would particularly encourage parents and grandparents to invite their children and grandchildren to read it before they get out of their teens. It is simple and profound. I pray that many people will encounter through this book the keys to discovering their God-given purpose.

Dr Allan Meyer

# Introduction

Why have I written this book?

I actually wrote the heart of this book some time ago, then decided to put it on the shelf unfinished.

After I spoke at a church recently a man came up to me and said that while I was speaking he felt the Lord had given him a message for me. He put it as a text on his phone. When he showed me, it read "Finish the Book". So here it is!

As a teenager my life was good. I loved my parents, sister, and relatives. I loved playing sport. I enjoyed cruising up and down the main street of my hometown in Horsham, Victoria, in my hotted up FJ Holden. Yet there was still something missing. There was an emptiness inside me.

I would often find myself asking the question "What's the purpose of my life?"

After I became a Christian, I discovered that my real purpose was to pursue the call of God upon my life.

I have based this book around the context of the following verse of Scripture in the book of Acts.

*'When he came and had seen the* **grace of God**, *he was glad and* **encouraged them all** *that with* **purpose of heart** *they should* **continue with the Lord'**.

Acts 11:23

Throughout the book, I have mixed sound biblical principles with experiences, and memoirs that I have encountered over many years in the ministry.

The book is formatted in such a way as to help the reader unlock their God-given purpose in life. It will appeal to all who seek to serve the Lord, especially those who aspire to be leaders and missionaries.

I'm talking about your spiritual gifting and passion. The thing that you get excited about, the thing that makes your eyes light up, and causes you to talk faster, the thing you want to pursue more than anything else.

I have gleaned stories from Australia, Papua New Guinea, Vanuatu, Indonesia, India, Borneo, Malaysia, Myanmar, Europe, UK and the USA.

Since retiring to the Gold Coast I have enjoyed the opportunity to do some Bible College Lecturing, Mentoring, and Ministry in some Churches. Also a little golfing, fishing, artwork, and lots of time with family and friends. I hope and pray that this book will help you to find your purpose in life and pursue it with a passion.

# SECTION 1

## Opening up your Heart

'...*that with* **purpose of heart** *they should continue with the Lord.*'

Acts 11:23

# Chapter 1
## Living with Shark Hunters

I have introduced this first chapter with a story I have written more in the form of a novel but based on historical facts. I have put this together as a result of my time spent among the 'Shark Callers of Kontu' in Papua New Guinea.

I am thankful to the late David Muap for sharing these traditional practices while I was with him in his home village of Kontu.

Kontu is a beautiful village on the West Coast of New Ireland, an island north of the mainland of PNG. It is fringed by deep blue lagoons. Freshwater springs bubble up through the stony beaches at low tide. It has a backdrop of dense green jungle and rugged mountain ranges.

As you will see this is all about a 'Change of Heart'

## UNLOCKING Your PURPOSE

Simbu climbed onto a rocky outcrop jutting up through the coral reef. He shook his thick black curly hair flinging sea water across his muscular shoulders. He paused for a moment to rest and soak up the warm tropical sun. Taking a fish from the end of his spear to use as shark bait, he smiled with satisfaction as he now had enough bait. He looked back toward his village surrounded by coconut palms and could see the smoke rising from early morning cooking fires.

With the tide coming in, he slid his canoe off the reef and began to paddle out to sea. It was now time for him to catch his first shark, kill it, bring it back to the village and eat the raw heart in front of everyone. This would mean that he would have a 'change of heart' taking on the nature of the shark and becoming a ferocious warrior in battle.

The small outrigger canoe rolled gently up and down with the ocean swell. He decided that he was far enough out to sea. In fact, he had never been this far out before. There were plenty of stories of others who had never returned from trying to catch they're first ever shark. When they killed a shark it was strapped to the side of the canoe. Often other sharks would attack and break up the canoe as they devoured the dead shark. Simbu tried to put these fears behind him.

He took up the round hoop with broken coconut shells attached to it and began to thrash the water to attract a shark. He did not have to wait long. A big shark slid under his canoe and began to circle. Simbu took the big wooden propeller with its noose threaded through the middle of it and hung it over the side of the canoe. He put a bait fish on a spear and slid it over the side poking it through the hangman like noose to attract the shark. The trap was set. The shark spotted the baitfish turned and lunged at it. Now the sharks head was in the noose.

Simbu quickly jerked the cord and threw the big propeller into the water. The shark was caught in the noose attached to the propeller. The propeller would spin around preventing the shark diving into the deep. There was no escape. All Simbu had to do was follow the spinning propeller and wait for the shark to become exhausted. Sensing the shark was tiring Simbu carefully paddled alongside the shark. He took a large club from his canoe and bashed it around the head until it was dead. He then took some vine and strapped the shark to the side of the canoe and began paddling back toward the shore.

When he was in sight of the village he took a large Trochus Shell, put it to his lips and gave some long blasts. This was to signal his success. He was elated to have made it back. A large crowd gathered on the shore to welcome him. It was a time of great joy and celebration. The shark was cut up and shared with the village. The heart was ceremoniously handed to Simbu who without hesitation began to eat the raw heart.

This tradition is still practiced today, except for eating the raw heart. While we were in the village the ABC was filming a documentary, now called 'The Shark Callers of Kontu'. The traditional equipment mentioned in this story can be seen in the Brisbane Museum.

## Our attempt to catch a shark

While we were in the village of Kontu, David and I decided we would 'give it a go'. No harm in trying to catch a shark by this traditional method. So we paddled out into the lagoon to catch some fish for bait. I stayed in the canoe, while David dived below, squeezing poison from a vine we had collected from the jungle, into cracks in the coral reef. The stunned fish that floated up to the surface I would grab and put in the canoe.

However, after a while, David became dizzy and sick from the effects of the poison, and I started to get seasick in the canoe. So we paddled back to shore somewhat embarrassed by our feeble attempt to catch a shark. I think all things were working together for good.

Not to be outdone the next day we set off into the jungle, with some village dogs, to hunt wild pigs with traditional spears. Another embarrassing story I would rather not talk about.

The very next day, early in the morning, David woke me up as he was whacking a bat to death. It was on a bunch of bananas hanging in our hut. With a big grin holding the bat up in victory David said: "Brother Terry, it's time to cook breakfast."

After this, I decided that we needed to stick to preaching the gospel.

## Opportunities to preach the gospel

We seized every opportunity to preach the gospel in Kontu, and the surrounding villages throughout the island. We proclaimed the need for a 'Change of Heart' by being born again, through accepting Christ as Lord and Saviour. We had a great response with many turning to Christ. Regardless of what nationality a person is, or the colour of their skin, or their cultural background, all have one common need, to repent of their sins and turn to Christ.

*'For **all have sinned** and fall short of the Glory of God'.*

Romans 3:23.

*'For the wages of **sin is death**, but the **gift of God is eternal life** in Jesus Christ our Lord'.*

## Life is no longer a Mystery

There was a mystery that had been kept hidden for centuries. It is now revealed to us and made clear through the coming of Christ.

*'...the **mystery** which has been **hidden** from ages and from generations, but has now been revealed to His saints. To them, God willed to make known what are the riches of the glory of this mystery among the Gentiles which is **Christ in you** the hope of glory.*

Colossians 1:26-28

Where do you fit in? Throughout this book, we will look at the keys to unlocking our purpose in life. Let's begin with the heart.

**UNLOCKING** Your **PURPOSE**

# Chapter 2
## Hidden Purposes within you

The things hidden in our hearts are deep and hard to fathom. These things need to be unlocked and brought to the surface if we are to discover and pursue our God-given purpose in Life. Our starting point is to open up our hearts to God and ask him to search out our hearts. What will He find?

> '*Search me* (thoroughly), *O God, and know my* **heart***! Try me and know my thoughts! And see if there is any wicked way in me...*'
>
> Psalm 139:23-24 (AMP)

I was raised in a family where we practiced a few traditional superstitions. Whenever we ate a roast chicken, the person who ended up with the wishbone made a secret wish. I can remember as a teenager making long wish lists but always ended up wishing I knew God. I was not a Christian at the time and I would be wondering where on earth that thought came from. It was concealed in my heart.

As a teenager, my mother would say "Terry I would not be surprised if you ended up in the ministry". What made her say that? Little did she realize how prophetic those words would become.

I had an old auntie who was a Spinster. One day as a teenager I was walking past her house and she was out the front and called me over and said she had something for me. She went inside and came out with this huge bible. She said, "Terry I won't be around much longer, I would like you to have this, I think you may be able to use it one day". It was in mint condition and printed back in the 1800s. I still have it. But out of all my cousins living in the same area, why did she want me to have it, I was not a religious person.

It was rare for me to go to church. I was sent to a Presbyterian Sunday School, and before we went out to lessons, we spent the first part of the service in the main church where the minister usually told a little story to the children. I still remember the day he pointed to one of the stain glass windows depicting Jesus standing at the door knocking, the caption at the bottom read "Behold I stand at the Door and Knock" Revelation 3:20. Then the minister looking at us said: "Do you notice there is one thing missing on the door?" After a moments silence he told us what it was, it was the door handle. He then launched into a mini message on when Jesus knocks on the door of your heart you have to open your heart from the inside and let him come in. I think that may have been the beginning of my heart opening up to Jesus.

## God has a purpose planned for you

We may be a mystery to ourselves, but not to God. He had our life mapped out for us from our mother's womb, from the very beginning we were made for a God-given purpose.

> *'You covered me in my **mother's womb**...Your eyes saw my substance, being yet unformed. And in your book, they were all written. **The days fashioned for me** when as yet there were none of them'.*
> Psalm 139:13-16

Surely this indicates that God has something planned for us from the womb. This is something that is concealed in our hearts. What can it be?

We are born in sin. This does not help because we live in a fallen world with demonic and evil influences that want to keep us in bondage.

We are often confronted with a sense of guilt and shame, and we feel we are not worthy of God's love and forgiveness. Our minds are often messed up with these thoughts and feelings.

> *'For as he **thinks** in his heart so he is'*
>
> Proverbs 23:7

## Christ now holds the key to your purpose

Only Christ can heal you and set you free to discover and pursue your God-given purpose in life. You need to start searching for Him with all of your heart.

> *'And you will seek Me and find Me when you* **search** *for Me with all your* **heart***'.*
>
> Jeremiah 29:13

In my early twenties, I would search for the evangelist Billy Graham on the radio or TV. When I heard him speak something would tug at my heart. When he gave the altar call I wished I was there.

Around that time a man by the name of Tony Smits came to my hometown in Horsham Victoria to pioneer a Christian Revival Crusade church, now replaced by the AOG church. We were working on a job together and he would witness to me and invite me to his meetings. I finally went along one night and gave my heart to the Lord. I was born again and my life dramatically changed.

I was still not sure how this would affect my life long term, all I knew at this stage was that I wanted to know more about God and serve him in some way. A lot of my friends did not understand what was happening, they just thought I had found religion. That was far from the truth I had found Christ and there is a big difference.

So within a short time, I met Caroline and we fell in love and she started coming to meetings. We told the Pastor that we wanted to get married. He gave us some good advice. He said we should be equally yoked together Body, Soul, and Spirit. In other words, apart from our Physical attraction

(Body), he suggested we be on a similar wavelength in our Thinking (Soul) and also in the realm of Spiritual Teaching (Spirit). I took it a step further, at the time I was baptised in the Holy Spirit and Caroline was not, so I waited until she was before we married. After we were married we headed off to the CRC Bible College in Adelaide. The College was being led by Dr Barry Chant, under the late Leo Harris.

## Delight yourself in the Lord

I have found that the more you desire to know God and the more you delight in Him and enjoy Him the more he seems to reveal Himself to you.

> *'Delight yourself in the Lord, and He will give you the desires and secret petitions of your heart'*
>
> Psalm 37:4 (AMP)

The word for 'delight' is from the Hebrew word 'anag' which simply means to be soft and pliable. If our heart remains soft and pliable as we seek to discover our God-given purpose in life He will surely reveal it to us. What desires and secret petitions do you have concealed in your heart? Stay soft and pliable and he will reveal them to you.

## Unlocking your Dreams

We all have hidden dreams locked away in our hearts. How can we fulfill those dreams? There may be several keys that will help us, but there is one that I have experienced over the years. It is to find the favour of God and man. We see this happening in many of the biblical stories. Let us take a look at Joseph. He had a special dream of his brothers bowing down to him. They didn't like the sound of it and sold him into slavery. He ended up in prison in Egypt. But he eventually found favour with the keeper of the prison.

> *'But the Lord was with Joseph and showed him mercy, and he gave him **favour** in the sight of the keeper of the prison.'*

> Genesis 39:21

Joseph was given authority over the prisoners. He gained a good reputation and through interpreting a dream that Pharaoh had gained favour with the Pharaoh and was made governor over Egypt.

> *'...and gave him **favour** and wisdom in the presence of Pharaoh, king of Egypt; and he made him governor over Egypt and all his house'.*

> Acts 7:10

Joseph eventually saw his dream fulfilled when his brothers came before him to buy grain because of a severe drought. They bowed before him before he revealed himself and embraced them.

The early church also initially found favour with people despite some persecution that was to follow.

> *'...praising God and having **favour** with all the people*

> Acts 2:47

As I look back over my life I realise that some of my dreams have been unlocked and fulfilled because of the favour of God and man. God has at times given me unexpected favour especially with key people who have helped me to see my dreams become reality. I would encourage you to seek God that he would grant you favour with people.

## Trust in the Lord with all your heart

As we walk with the Lord we need to learn to trust Him with all our heart.

*'**Trust** in the **Lord** with all your **heart** and lean not on your own understanding'.*

Proverbs 3:5

This is not a suggestion, it is a decree. It reveals God's desire for us. He wants us to have faith and confidence in Him at all times. Regardless of circumstances, we do not understand, we are to trust Him with all of our heart.

As you continue to read this book, hopefully, it will help you in the process of unlocking and discovering your purpose in life.

**UNLOCKING** Your **PURPOSE**

# Chapter 3
## Is your heart in it?

Is your heart really in whatever you are doing in life? Or are you still trying to figure it out?

When I first started in full-time ministry as an assistant pastor to Hal Oxley, at Life Ministry Centre, in Melbourne, he asked me if I would take over some of the church administration. Hal had been a Colonel in the army, deputy head of Military Intelligence, and a Manufacturer, before entering the ministry. I knew my administrative skills would never measure up. So I declined, knowing that my heart would not be in it. After further discussion, I was appointed to more of a Pastoral role. This included Shepherding, Counselling, Visitation, Home Groups, and so on. My heart was in it because it was more in keeping with my pastoral gifting. As a result, my life was very fruitful and enjoyable at the time. The administration would have become a source of frustration for me and everyone around me. Today this great church is being led by Graham and Chris Nelson. Graham is a brilliant leader and administrator.

When our heart is in something we find the energy and enthusiasm that is required to fulfil our calling. It becomes a joy, and we seem to be able to extend ourselves beyond our natural capabilities. We end up being able to accomplish much more than we ever thought possible.

## More than just Duty

I heard someone preach a message on serving the Lord out of Duty. It was based on Luke 17:10 'We are unprofitable servants. We have done what was our duty to do'. The message disturbed me though because the preacher kept labouring the point. We should serve the Lord out of duty whether our heart was in it or not. He was trying to inspire us to serve because it was our duty to serve. This, in turn, would prove our loyalty and commitment to the Lord.

I thought to myself, what about serving from the heart? I know we all go through times when it may feel that we are serving out of duty. Sometimes it seems as though we are just going through the motions. But this was not being said by the preacher.

I started thinking of the dangers of serving just out of duty. One would become cold, hard and indifferent. It could lead to a dull and boring life. It may affect our relationship with the Lord and His people. Our ministry would become a mere formality. Just another job, rather than a calling.

There would be little room for creativity, and for the leading and moving of the Holy Spirit in all that we were called to do in ministry.

## What are you Called to do?

What inspires you? What are you called to do in life? Is it secular or is it some form of ministry?

You may feel called to a Professional career, or be a Tradesperson, a Salesperson, a Shop Assistant, a Politician, a Farmer, or manage a Business of your own. If it is something you enjoy doing and you love it, and you feel the Lord is in it, then keep pursuing it. There are many dedicated Christians serving in a secular capacity who help support the ministry. In fact, without their support, it would be hard to stay in ministry. Many pastors in smaller churches have part-time jobs to survive in ministry.

## It makes a difference when your heart is in it!

One area we find difficult at times is that of giving. But what a difference it makes when our heart is in it. This can be a real challenge for most of us.

> '*So let each one gives as he **purposes in his heart**, not grudgingly or of necessity; for God loves a cheerful giver.*'
>
> 1 Corinthians 9:7

The heart is at the centre of our emotions. The heart that is hurt or wounded needs to be made whole. I have ministered to many people who have been deeply wounded in some way. The heart is often the foundation for our emotions and attitudes in life. Our heart shapes who we are and what we will be. It is the driving force of our life. It is at the very core of our being. Therefore we really do need to take good care of it.

> '*Keep your **heart with all diligence** for out of it springs the issues of life*'.
>
> Proverbs 4:23

## What drives you to do what you do?

It may be family, friends, peers, business, money, sport, pleasure, tradition, or something else. There is nothing wrong with these things. In some cases, they could be motivating factors that drive you to do what you do. When I was playing a sport it was my close friends or the team members that inspired me to do what I did to the best of my ability.

When it comes to serving the lord you need to begin to seek Him for a specific purpose. Ask Him to reveal His desires for you in your heart. This will help you to eventually discover your God-given purpose and enable you to pursue it with enthusiasm. You will need to be sensitive to the leading of the Holy Spirit to see this outworked in your life. The apostle Paul was always open to the leading of the Holy Spirit.

> '*Paul **purposed** in the **Spirit** when he had passed through Macedonia and Achaia, to go to Jerusalem*'.
>
> Acts 19:21

My understanding of the 'Greek' for the phrase 'purposed in the Spirit' is that he 'settled' it in his heart to go.

## Speak about what is in your heart

You need to get excited and talk about what is in your heart. When God births something in your heart it is very hard to keep quiet about it.

*'...for out of the abundance of the **heart** the mouth speaks'.*

Matthew 12: 35-37

## Catching some fire from others as they speak

I love being around people who talk excitedly about the things that God has put in their heart.

I always enjoy fellowshipping with the likes of Dr Allan Meyer who cannot help but talk about the things that God has placed in his heart. Allan is a good friend, and one of the best communicators I know. I love his preaching. He is so expressive and inspiring. He is no different when you are talking to him on a personal level. He lights a fire in your heart. Allan and his wife Helen are founders of 'Careforce Lifekeys'.

I met up with pastor Jack Hanes while we were holidaying on the Gold Coast. He was staying in the same apartment block and we ended up playing golf together on several occasions. At the time Jack had been appointed the head of missions for the AOG. Jack always talked with great enthusiasm. He spoke freely of the things that God had put in his heart. Those things had a profound impact on my life and ministry at the time. Jack and his church in Sydney later sponsored me on a trip to Budapest, in Hungary, to minister there together with Eugene Bognar, who is like an apostle to that nation.

While in PNG John and Coby Pasterkamp were very hospitable. John had a lovely spirit, he would share his thoughts and insights with you and had a way of making you feel great. He was able to warm your heart as he spoke with you.

In Lismore, my associate Rod Dymock and I would spend time together talking about doctrine and Church and College-related issues. I was always encouraged in my heart by Rod's insight, wisdom, practicality, and grace.

These days, I enjoy a round of golf with Tony Hughes, Tony and his wife Nina were missionaries in Russia and Kiev, in the Ukraine. Tony and I always have some stimulating heart-stirring theological discussions.

Talking with others can be a bit like the disciples on the road to Emmaus who after talking with Jesus said to one another.

*'...did not our **hearts burn** within us'*

Luke 24:32

After talking to some people our hearts can burn within us. It is as though the Lord has used them to inspire us to pursue our purpose. So it is good to be around people who talk about their purpose of heart.

**UNLOCKING** Your **PURPOSE**

# Chapter 4
## Avoid living without a Purpose

We can live life with or without a purpose. The choice is ours. My experience has been that people who live life with a purpose seem far more fulfilled than those who appear to have no purpose.

Without a purpose, life seems to be pointless. We feel like a ship without a rudder. Just drifting along from day to day. Life is empty and meaningless.

You only have to read the book of Ecclesiastes to see that life without a purpose is futile and vain.

> *'Vanity of vanities, all is **vanity**. What profit does a man have from all his labour?'*
>
> Ecclesiastes 1:2-3

This theme continues throughout the book. It is almost

depressive to read until you realize he is trying to get a point across. That life without God is extremely shallow and empty. He redeems himself in the last few verses where he makes a summary and concludes with the answer to life.

> *'Fear God and keep His commandments, for this is the whole duty **(purpose)** of man'*
>
> Ecclesiastes 12:13

## Discovering Spiritual Values

I had the privilege of meeting Bernard Dowd, just before he died. He was chief of Dowd Associates the manufacturer of 'Hickory' Lingerie in Australia, they sponsored the 'Miss Australia' quest for years. He was a very wealthy man. After he became a Christian together with other family members, knowing he was dying, he made this statement "I have had everything that life has to offer, but the one thing that has eluded me, has been true happiness, now I believe I have found it in Christ".

The thing is, when we turn to Christ we see things from a vastly different perspective. We discover spiritual values that we never knew existed. We then need to find out where and how we fit in. You may end up serving the Lord in an area that exceeds your natural talents and abilities. You could become a Pastor, an Apostle, a Teacher, a Prophet, an Evangelist, or perhaps an Elder, a Deacon, a Musician, a Singer, or a Helper in the church in some special way.

I remember a man on the door to greet people when we

were serving in Melbourne. It was worth going to church just to receive his enthusiastic warm welcome. He greeted everyone with the same love and acceptance and it really made you feel great. It was his ministry.

I hope this book will unlock spiritual values for you, and help you to discover your calling and ministry in life.

## Jesus gives us a higher Purpose in Life

When Jesus called his disciples to follow Him He immediately gave them a higher purpose in life.

When He saw Simon and Andrew his brother who were professional fishermen, He said to them *"Come after Me, and I will make you become fishers of men"*. Mark 1:16-17.

They knew all about catching fish. Now Jesus presents them with a higher purpose. To make them become 'fishers of men'. The Messiah was not just asking them to follow Him. He was presenting them with a challenging proposal. What an opportunity! A higher purpose they could put their heart into, a purpose that added more meaning to life, it would not only change their lives but also one that would change the destiny of the whole world.

Jesus reassures them of this higher purpose when he tells Peter "let down your nets for a catch" Peter replies "We have fished all night and caught nothing but nevertheless, at your word I will let down the net". As a result, they caught so many fish they had to call on their partners to come and help them. Jesus said to them;

> *'Do not be afraid. From now on you will **catch men**'.*
>
> Luke 5:10

Maybe this was a foretaste of the future harvest that they were about to encounter.

## Offenses may hinder us pursuing our Purpose

We can sometimes become offended for one reason or another. This can hinder us from pursuing our God-given purpose. I have spoken to a number of people that have become offended, often over minor issues, usually something somebody has said or done. Unfortunately, some are no longer serving the Lord or attending church.

Even those who were close to Christ became offended with Him. There was a time when many of His disciples were offended by His teaching and turned away from following Him.

> *'…from that time many of His disciples went back **and walked with Him no more**'.*
>
> John 6:66

It's hard to believe, but they walked with Him no more. What did they go back to? Probably back to whatever they were doing before. It is sad to think that someone can stop pursuing their God-given purpose over something that has offended them.

Jesus warns us that 'offense' will be something that we will face in the last days.

> *'And many will be **offended**, will betray one another, and will hate one another'.*
>
> Matthew 24:10

May we not become offended by some misunderstanding or something somebody has said or done to upset us and turn away from following Christ.

## Facing Retirement with or without a Purpose

I felt the time was right to retire. But facing retirement without a purpose was a scary reality. I felt I still had something to contribute but could not work out what that might look like. So I decided to leave it up to the Lord and went ahead and retired to the Gold Coast.

We continued with our alliance to A2A, which was being led by Philip Mutzelburg, who was also leading the influential 'Catalyst Church' in Ipswich. Philip and Mandy have handed the church over to their son Carl and his wife Jessica. At the time of writing A2A is now being led by Tim O'Neill. Tim and his wife Sharon lead the impressive 'Trailrace Community Centre' in Launceston, Tasmania.

We initially fellowshipped at 'Church One' with Pastor Ted and Amanda Pangilinan. During that time I became a lecturer at Dunamis Bible College in Brisbane, under the leadership of Pastor Shaun and Sandra Hansen. I also spent time mentoring some A2A Pastors. It was a fruitful and fulfilling time. It continued to give me a purpose.

We were then approached by Denis and Lois Barnard to help out with ministry at 'Meadowbrook Christian Church' in Brisbane. They had purchased a property and had built a church on it which was having an impact in that community. However, they eventually retired and handed over to Pastor George and Angie Gebran. George has a great team and has taken the church to another level. He has also been gracious enough to allow me to continue to assist in ministering in that church.

I also joined Volunteer Marine Rescue (VMR). I enjoy playing Golf, Fishing, and Art. Most of all, my wife and I enjoy spending time with our children and grandchildren. So we still feel we have a worthwhile purpose to pursue.

### I still get things to share

In my retirement, I still get things to share.

It was Boaz that told his men to purposely leave grain fall to the ground for Ruth to pick up.

*'Also let **grain** from the bundles fall **purposely** for her'.*

Ruth 2:16

I feel at times the Lord gives me understanding in the word in seed form. It may come through listening to others or private study. It is almost as though it is on purpose for a purpose. I still find myself gathering studies and sermons in seed form. Maybe its habit after doing it for years.

In any case, I still hope that as long as I live I will always have something to share. I feel this book is a part of me fulfilling my purpose in life at this time and I pray that it will also help others to fulfill their purpose.

# SECTION 2
## Opening up your Gifting

*'When he came and saw* **the grace of God** *he was glad...'*

Acts 11:23

# Chapter 5
## Grace for your Purpose

The grace of God allows you to unlock and open up whatever possibilities you may have concerning your purpose in life. You can afford to experiment while you work out just what your God-given purpose may be.

When Barnabas came to Antioch and saw the grace of God he was glad. Why was that? Because he did not find believers bound by the law or the religious traditions of men. He found believers that had embraced the grace of God and were free to discover and pursue their purpose.

Robert Farrar Capon, says in his book 'Kingdom, Grace, Judgement'.

*'The church is not in the religion business. It never has been and never will be. The church is in the Gospel-proclaiming business. It is not here to bring bad news but Good News that "while we were yet sinners Christ died for the ungodly". It is here in short for no*

*religious purpose at all, only to announce the Gospel of free grace'.*

I believe we need a fresh understanding of the grace of God in the church today.

## Grace concealed in the Gospels

Many of the encounters and parables recorded in the Gospels and told by Jesus, reveal to us the grace of God. They expose self-righteous efforts and religious traditions to try and please God, as being completely inadequate. For example, the man that came to Jesus asking "Good Teacher, What shall I do that I may inherit eternal life?" Jesus replied

*"Why do you call me **good**?*
*No one is **good** but one, that is, **God**.*

Mark 10:17-22

Does this mean Jesus was not good? Of course not, He was trying to make a point. Then Jesus goes on to mention the commandments to which this man responds that he has kept them all from his youth. Jesus was impressed, this man was indeed a good man. Jesus then says there is one thing you lack go and sell what you have, take up your cross and follow me. This man went away sad for he had great possessions.

So this is the point Jesus is trying to make. That no matter how good we may be, or how hard we may try, that our goodness, is not good enough to inherit eternal life. It is not our goodness, but God's goodness that leads us to repentance and eternal life. It is not based on our performance or our works, but the grace of God. Throughout the gospels, we have similar encounters that reveal to us the importance of the grace of God.

I recently came across a busload of men from Toowoomba. They all had the same coloured tee shirts on with the logo across the front that read "Wanabees Social Club". Curiosity got the better of me, so I asked what the "Wanabees" stood for. They replied that they were a group of golfers that were not good, but they "wana be good". I thought to myself there are a lot of Christians in that category. They see themselves as not being good and are forever striving to be good by their own self-righteous works rather than relying on the grace of God.

## A lack of Grace brings judgement

I was playing golf with my son Andrew. He was my partner and we were in a foursome competition. I was having a really bad round. Suddenly my son turned and said to me "Dad there must be sin in your life". His lack of grace brought judgement upon me. It did not help my game, I went from bad to worse. He really surprised me as he is usually so gracious. I am very proud of Andrew today. He is far more gracious. At the time of writing, he is an Engineer and a part-time Baptist Minister, at the 'Fairfield Christian Family Church' in Brisbane.

Some time ago my wife fell over and broke her leg. I remember a pastor at the time telling her to believe God and get rid of the plaster. He came across hard and indifferent. A few months later we ran into the same pastor wearing a plaster cast. We reframed from our tendency to want to pass judgement on him. We showed grace and offered a prayer for his recovery.

The apostle Paul says we need to be careful not to become proud or arrogant when we consider our calling and purpose in life.

> '...*God chose what is low and despised in the world, even things that are not, to bring to nothing things that are, so that* **no human being might boast** *in the presence of God*'
>
> 1 Corinthians 1:26-29

Even though the apostle Paul was a brilliant man in the natural he was aware of the dangers of pride and had become dependent upon the grace of God.

## We are so dependent upon the grace of God

The grace of God will not only help us to find a purpose but also give us the freedom to pursue it. It is difficult to follow a God-given purpose if our heart is all cluttered up with tradition and legalism. We will probably stumble trying to please those who demand we follow certain traditional practices that are not directly related to the call of God upon our lives. This brings us into bondage, not freedom.

The Apostle Paul with his strict religious background became so dependent upon the grace of God to pursue his calling.

'**I am not worthy to be called an apostle**, *because I*

*persecuted the church of God. But by the **grace of God**, I am what I am, and His grace toward me was not in vain'.*

1 Corinthians 15:9-10

Also when Paul encountered difficulties God showed him that he would get through the hard times because of the Grace of God. When Paul was struggling and afflicted by a 'thorn in the flesh'. God assured him by saying.

*'My **grace is sufficient** for you, for my strength is made perfect in Weakness'.*

2 Corinthians 12:9

Yes, we are all so dependent upon the grace of God to survive in ministry and follow our calling.

## Never give in or give up

There have been times when I wanted to give in or give up because things were really tough. At times I felt like resigning from the ministry. I was never able to put pen to paper. I believe it was the grace of God that enabled me to keep going while under pressure. When I felt I was facing defeat God would step in and turn things around.

If you are in a situation where you feel like quitting, keep going. Do not give in or give up. Like Churchill would say during the Second World War "We will never surrender". You are never defeated until you say you are. Speak words of victory not defeat.

The grace of God enables us to reign in life.

*'...those who receive abundance of **grace** and of **the gift** of righteousness will **reign** in life through the One, Jesus Christ'.*

Romans 5:17

The words of the Hymn 'Amazing Grace' are so good. "Tis grace that brought me safe thus far and grace will lead me home". This is twofold. Firstly, we are where we are today because of His Amazing Grace. His grace has brought us this far. Secondly, we can have confidence that His grace will not fail us in the future. His grace will also lead us home or on into Eternity.

## Grace opens up all kinds of possibilities

The grace of God opens up possibilities that help us to surpass our natural gifts and talents. When I look back over my life I am amazed by some of the things that the Lord has enabled me to do. When I was younger I was very shy and would never have dreamt of entering the ministry. By His grace, I have accomplished much more than I thought possible. I once preached a series on grace. Things began to happen. A lady who had been wearing a back brace to bed for years was miraculously healed. Preaching on grace, released faith and helped some people to step into the grace of God and believe for miracles.

## We still need the Spiritual Disciplines

Grace is no excuse for becoming lazy. We are not saved

by them, but Spiritual Disciplines such as Bible Study, Prayer, Fasting, Worship, Fellowship, Giving and so on, are all necessary for our spiritual development as we journey through life.

## A fresh wave of grace

A number of ministers today have a fresh revelation of the grace of God. John Latta a good friend of mine has an exceptional understanding of the grace of God and loves to preach on grace. John and his wife Jill are the leaders of the Tweed Heads Church of Christ.

The foundation of the early Christian Church was built upon grace. It seems that in the last days there will be a fresh wave of grace to cap things off.

> *'...and He shall bring forth the **capstone** with shouts of **grace**, grace to it'.*
>
> Zechariah 4:6-7

**UNLOCKING** Your **PURPOSE**

# Chapter 6
## Discovering Your Gifting

It may take time to fully unlock and discover your gifting. As stated in the previous chapter, grace helps you to process what that might eventually look like. Your gifting should connect you to your purpose. Where do you begin? Apart from the simple answer of by being led by the Holy Spirit, I would suggest that the grace of God also has a vital role to play when it comes to discovering your gifting.

A study of what I have termed as the 'grace gifts' as mentioned in Romans 12 has helped me to clarify my basic gifting. It has also given me insight into the way other people function and what their basic gifting may be. A balanced look at these gifts of grace will usually help us to discern what shape our gifting may take in the future.

### Firstly, renewing the mind for a purpose

> *'but be transformed by the renewing of your mind that you may prove what is that good and acceptable and perfect **will of God**'.*

Romans 12:2

This verse is often preached separately from the following verses. If we look at the context it is meant to help us find what the will of God is for our lives. I would suggest that this verse is leading us to explore the 'grace gifts' that are listed to enable us to find the will of God for our lives.

So Paul is not just telling us to renew our minds to get away from the influence of the world. He's asking us to do this to go on and discover what the will of God is for our life by studying the gifts of grace. This will, in turn, help us to discover our basic gifting.

## Secondly, some things to seriously consider

Leading into the 'grace gifts', we are encouraged to seriously evaluate some important things about ourselves so that we end up with a balanced view of ourselves. It is no good overestimating our gifting and abilities. If we do that we step outside of the grace of God that we need to function effectively.

> *'to everyone who is among you **not to think of himself more highly** than he ought to think, but to **think soberly**, as God has dealt to each one a **measure of faith**, for we are many members in one body, but all the members do **not have the same function**'.*

Rom 12:3-6

There are several things mentioned in these verses. We are to give some serious thought to these in the context of our purpose and function within the life of the church.

1. To think soberly about our Abilities.

2. To think about our Measure of Faith.

3. To think about our Function in the Body.

We would do well to think about these things in the context of how we function in the 'grace gifts'.

## Thirdly, identifying with the Grace Gifts

We will probably discover that we can identify with one of these basic gifts, maybe more. Although one usually seems to fit us more than others.

> 'Having then **gifts differing** according to the **grace given to us**, let us use them; if Prophecy, let us prophesy in proportion to our faith, or Ministry, let us use it in our ministering; he who Teaches in teaching; he who Exhorts in exhortation; he who Gives with liberality; he who Leads with diligence; he who shows Mercy, with cheerfulness.
>
> Romans 12:6-8

The seven grace gifts mentioned here are -

1. Prophecy (also refers to speaking)

2. Ministry (this has more to do with serving)

3. Teaching (the ability to explain truth)

4. Exhorting (this has to do with encouraging)

5. Giving (giving of resources and time)

6. Leadership (this is the ability to lead others)

7. Mercy (to come alongside those in need)

These are basic gifts. Divine abilities are given to us by the grace of God. When you discover what gift fits you it will make sense. It is something you will be inclined to do without much effort. It will just seem to fit in with your personality. My associate in Lismore, Rod Dymock has a teaching gift and uses lots of points to make a point. In my office one day, using algebra, he tried to explain how they put a man on the moon. My mind just doesn't work that way. I'm not so precise, I'm more of an inspirational prophetic teacher that likes to encourage.

## Discerning what is an authentic gift

Does a person have an authentic gift or not? It is sometimes hard to discern, but I have found that the inner witness of the Holy Spirit gives us discernment. Sometimes we have people trying so hard to flow in a gift that does not fit them. They may even be a way off track.

I was worshiping one Sunday morning in the front row of our church in Lismore. Suddenly I felt a presence in front of me. I opened my eyes to find a young lady I had never seen before staring up into my face. She said, "I have a message for the Church, I am the angel grace out of the book of revelation." I said, "No you are not, now go and sit down". She did but quickly disappeared out the door before the end of the meeting. This is an extreme case. Others are more subtle they first appear to be okay, until they really step out of line, causing confusion by what they say or do.

## Other gifts to also consider

The grace gifts are only a basic guide to what our ministry gift may look like. We should also see if our ministry lines up with the five-fold ministry gifts mentioned in Ephesians 4. The function of the gifts of the Holy Spirit as listed in 1 Corinthians 12 in our ministry should also help define our gifting.

The important thing is that we discover and pursue our purpose and function in the gift that we are comfortable in.

## Trial and Error

If we are not sure about our gifting and purpose of heart. There is always the principle of trial and error. Sometimes we just need to experiment and 'give it a go'. In other words, if you think you are gifted in a certain area get involved and see how it works out. In Lismore, I was so blessed to have such talented associates as Rod and Margaret Dymock. Margaret led a successful 'Youth Music' group that was open to all the youth to come and have a go. It was basically trial and error for many but produced some tremendous talent.

If it is your gifting it will flow and not be a burden. It will be easy, a real joy. It will give you a buzz, and you will feel fulfilled. When it is not your gifting it will be hard work and a real burden to you. Jesus said

> '*Come unto Me all you that labour and are heavy laden, and I will give you rest.* **Take My yoke upon you** *and learn from Me…For My yoke is easy and My burden is* **light**'.
>
> Matthew 11:28-29

To me, this speaks not just to believers in general, but also to all those who desire to serve in some way. There will be times of stress, but generally speaking, if God is in what we do, it should not be a heavy load that we cannot bear.

I would encourage you to embrace the grace of God, study the 'grace gifts', and use this as a platform to discover your gifting and purpose.

# Chapter 7
## Faith to pursue your Purpose

We need faith to unlock and pursue our purpose. Without faith, we would probably cave in under pressure and give up on pursuing our purpose.

**Faith 'Born of the Spirit'**

Faith born of the Spirit will help us to overcome whatever obstacles we face in life.

*'For **whatever is born** of God overcomes the world. And this is the victory that has overcome the world – our **Faith**'.*

1John 5:4

It says 'whatever' is born of God. However, in verse one we read 'whoever' is born of God. So I would suggest that 'whoever' is born of God also needs a 'whatever' is born of God to have faith to overcome when facing difficult situations.

When we went to the mission field we had a 'whatever' that was born of God based on Jeremiah 1:4-10 which was also supported by a prophetic word. Without that word born of the Spirit we probably would have given up. While a Bible College was being built in Port Moresby we started lectures at a Scout Camp up in the hills. The conditions were terrible. We were surrounded by jungle and mosquitoes.

We also had no home while one was being built for us on the Bible College property. During this time we had to rely on 'Leave Houses'. When people went on leave they wanted someone in their house while they were gone to keep it secure from invasion by rascal gangs. We were in transit as a family. We had six moves in twelve months. Thank God we had a word of faith born of the Spirit that enabled us to overcome these difficulties.

Despite many personal trials the church still grew from about 120 to around 500 over a six-year period. Hardly a week went by without people being saved. It was a time of revival all over the nation. Many were saved, healed, delivered and filled with the Holy Spirit.

I usually ask the Lord for a word born of the Spirit before making a major decision to pursue a particular purpose. On one occasion, without a word born of the Spirit, I thought the Lord may have been calling us to Launceston in Tasmania. So I flew to Launceston, but as soon as the plane landed I felt the Lord say "No, this is not for you". It seemed as though the Lord used the trip to guide me and also get the thought out of my system.

## A prophetic word can impart faith

I have had many prophetic words that have imparted faith. Two such words stand out. One from Kindah Greening saying that I would be like a statesman to bring the word to a disadvantaged nation. I believe that was fulfilled while we were in PNG. On one occasion we had the privilege of meeting the then Prime Minister Sir Michael Somare for morning tea. At other times we met other officials in high places.

The other word was more on a personal level from the late Peter Morrow. His was more along the line of not being discouraged by hard situations because God was putting steel into my spirit. This was to enable me to endure trials and strengthen my faith to stand against the powers of darkness.

I do not like to prophesy anything negative over people. But, on one occasion on the island of Bougainville, while ministering with Barry Winton at a leaders meeting, I gave a prophecy over a national leader. I said that he would face persecution but that it would work out for good in the end.

I later heard that when he returned to his village he was severely beaten. Apparently, that word of prophecy had given him faith to continue to minister. He later saw some of his persecutors turn to the Lord. His church grew and had an impact in that particular area.

## Smuggling Bibles into Myanmar

Fear is one of our biggest hindrances to our faith. I had been invited to minister in Hyderabad in India. I was traveling with Denis Barnard. We had an over night stop in Bangkok, where we met someone to arrange for us to smuggle Bibles into Myanmar. We were given a lot of various size packages (wrapped up bibles) to look like gifts in our luggage. We were provided with return tickets so we could resume our journey to India. We were told we would be okay as long as our luggage was not X-rayed.

That night I had a terrible dream (nightmare) in my dream I had been caught for smuggling Bibles and stood against a wall to be shot. I remember a soldier offered me a cigarette, but I said: "No thanks I don't smoke". I woke up in a cold sweat, fear gripping my heart.

I sought the Lord for a word of faith, God gave me;

*'**Fear not**, for I am with you; be not dismayed for I am your God. I will strengthen you, Yes, I will help you...'*

*Isaiah 41:10*

I sure needed that word. When the plane landed an announcement was made that all luggage would be X-rayed. All the time meditating upon that word we did the necessary paperwork at the customs counter, then headed toward the X-ray machine. To our surprise, an official ushered us away from the machine and out the exit door.

## Doubt undermines our faith

When Peter saw Jesus walking on the water he also wanted to give it a go, Jesus gave him the okay and told him to come.

But when Peter saw how boisterous the wind was blowing he began to sink and cried out for the Lord to save him.

> *'...Jesus stretched out his hand and caught him, and said to him, "Oh you of little faith, **why did you doubt?**'.*
>
> Matthew 14:31

Jesus pinpointed the problem when he said to Peter "Why did you doubt?" Peter was in two minds. In the book of James, we have a reminder of how doubt can rob us of our faith.

> *'...for he who **doubts** is like a wave of the sea driven and tossed by the wind. For let, not that man suppose that he will receive anything from the Lord'.*
>
> *James 1:6-8*

I wanted to take my family on a 'Bare Boat Charter' holiday in the Whitsunday Islands. I was in two minds. I doubted my ability to handle a 35ft Cruiser when my only experience was pottering around in a 12ft Tinnie. I decided to step out in faith and give it a go. When we left Shute Harbour we ran into a strong wind blowing down the Whitsunday passage and a big swell. My doubts and my family were prompting me to turn back. But my faith rose to the challenge and we made it across to Nara Inlet. Doubt almost robbed us of a wonderful holiday.

## A Word of faith for a special purpose

When we have a word of faith born of the Spirit it is often for a special purpose. Our great example can be found in the story of Abraham and Sarah who were childless. However, God promised them that they would have an heir but it did not happen until they were too old in the natural to have a child. They believed God and were commended for their faith.

> *'Abraham did not waver at the promise of God through unbelief, but was strengthened in **faith**, giving glory to God, and being **fully convinced** that what He had promised, He was also able to perform'.*
>
> Romans 4:20-22

When we have a word of faith that is born of the Spirit, it helps us to focus on the purpose for which that word was given. It will help us to be convinced that God is in that purpose and that it will come to pass.

## 'By faith' in Hebrews 11

By faith, these men and women all accomplished great things. They all had one thing in common. They had a word from God, born of the Spirit.

Most of them were able to overcome persecution, adversity, and opposition because they had a word from God. It was that word that enabled them to have faith to fulfill the purpose that God had for them.

## Our faith will be tested

Our faith is usually put to the test. At the time of traveling to the tropics, our then three-year-old daughter Felicity had suffered a series of convulsions. We would have to cool her down with cold water and put a fan on her. We were in two minds about going. But we had a word born of the Spirit. This would test our faith. Hot humid weather, the danger of contracting Malaria, and having limited medical facilities, none of these thoughts helped our faith. We went because we had a word of faith born of the Spirit.

We were fortunate, apart from Felicity having one convulsion, we had no more problems with her. Also by the grace of God, none of us contracted Malaria.

We have endured many trials that have tested our faith over the years we have been in ministry.

> *'...greatly rejoice, though now for a little while, if need be, you have been grieved by **various trials**, that the **genuineness of your faith**, being much more precious than gold that perishes, though it be tested by fire...'*
>
> 1 Peter 1:6-7

Yes, when we pursue a purpose in faith it will be put to the test. But God is faithful to bring us through those times that we might fulfill our purpose.

**UNLOCKING** Your **PURPOSE**

# Chapter 8
## Inspired by Good Leaders

We all need to be inspired by good leaders. I still remember some of the very first leaders who encouraged me in ministry. Their input into my life was crucial at the time. They helped to unlock my purpose and inspired me to pursue it.

We read that Barnabas was a good man. His name means 'Son of Encouragement'. This was one of his most important characteristics. He was able to encourage believers to serve the Lord. In Acts 4:36-37 Barnabas is first mentioned as a land owner who sold some land and generously donated the proceeds to the apostles at Jerusalem.

### Good men are often bold in Spirit

Barnabas was not only a good man but a bold man, full of the Holy Spirit and Faith. Together with Paul in Acts 14:3 we read of their boldness.

'They were speaking **boldly** in the Lord, who was bearing witness to the word of his grace, granting *signs and wonders* to be done by their hands'.

Signs and wonders were done by their hands. They had a boldness in the Spirit. I have observed over the years that good leaders usually have a boldness to believe for Signs and Wonders.

I have been inspired by ministering alongside many good leaders who have had a boldness in the Spirit. I could name several, but one, in particular, comes to mind. The late Derek Prince.

## Assisting the late Derek Prince

I was given the opportunity to assist the late Derek Prince in some of his mass deliverance meetings held in Melbourne. I was amazed at his boldness and authority in those meetings. As a young pastor, I was freaked out by some of the demonic manifestations. I was way out of my depth. I made sure I stayed close to Derek. This experience came in handy later, especially on the mission field as I encountered many demonic manifestations.

## Mentored and Inspired by many good men

I have been mentored and inspired by many good men over a long period of time. I started to list them and ended up with a full page of names. So in case, I missed someone, I deleted the list. It takes a number of good leaders from different backgrounds to impact our lives.

My advice would be to aspiring leaders not to limit themselves to just a few good men. We were visiting a church on holidays. After the meeting, we went into their bookshop. It was reasonably well stocked but was limited to just four different authors. We really do need a greater representation from the whole body of Christ.

## Good leaders have good working relationships

Good leaders have good working relationships in their own church, and with other church leaders.

As a visiting minister, I was picked up from the airport by the local pastor. When we drove past the Catholic Church in his town he pointed to it and said to me "Mystery Babylon the Great Mother of Harlots". I knew he was quoting from the book of revelation. I was shocked. I later found out that he had some bad attitudes toward other churches. He did not value good working relationships with others. His church suffered because of his bias.

When we were on the mission field we endeavoured to do everything we could to have good working relationships with other missions and missionaries. We benefitted by being able to hold combined leaders meetings and outreaches together.

When we were in Lismore we enjoyed fellowshipping with the Ministers Fraternal. We met on a regular basis and held combined Church Meetings. We may not have agreed on some doctrinal issues. But for the sake of unity, we put them aside.

> *'...endeavouring to keep the **unity of the Spirit** in the bond of peace'*
>
> Ephesians 4:3

Good leaders will keep the unity of the Spirit because they have a common purpose. Promoting and proclaiming the Gospel.

## Small beginnings make good leaders

Good leaders often start with small beginnings and endure some tough times before growing and developing into really good leaders.

> *'For who has **despised** the day of **small** things?'*
>
> Zechariah 4:10

When I first began in ministry I began pioneering in a small country area in the hills on the outskirts of Melbourne. We advertised meetings to be held in a Scout hall on a Saturday night and on a Sunday morning. My wife and I would try and make the hall presentable by scraping up cigarette butts, and mopping the floor, and setting up chairs. We would then go and door knock handing out invitations to our meetings. A few people responded.

After one Saturday night, we had no one turn up. I became discouraged and was ready to quit. I complained and said to the Lord "This is the end for me". I then opened my bible randomly and it fell open in Ezekiel and I read "The end is not yet".

So I continued and the next morning we had several attend. After a while, we were getting around forty regulars and I handed over to someone else.

I was then invited to join the ministry team at Life Ministry Centre, in those days it was a large church in Melbourne.

We should never despise small beginnings for everything in life begins in seed form, it then grows and matures as it grows.

Dietrich Bonhoeffer in his book 'The Cost of Discipleship' says "Small beginnings is how the church invades the life of the world and conquers territory for Christ".

We need to overcome being discouraged by small beginnings and small numbers. We are laying a foundation for growth and better things to come.

## It takes vision and faith to inspire others

Good leaders will inspire others with vision and faith. They are able to cast a vision that inspires people to want to be a part of that vision and they will desire to support it. They are leaders pursuing a God-given Purpose.

Oswald J. Sanders in his book 'Spiritual leadership' speaks of the impact of those with faith and vision.

'Those who have most powerfully and permanently influenced their generation have been the seers-those who have seen more and further than others-men of faith, for faith is vision'.

Church elders also need to be people of faith.

*'For by it (**faith**), the elders obtained a good testimony'.*

Hebrews 11:2

## We should not lord it over the Flock

Good leaders will not lord it over the flock. They will be able to lead with grace and dignity. If they are good shepherds over the flock, people will desire to follow them.

*'**Shepherd** the flock of God which is among you, serving as overseers...**nor as being lords** over those entrusted to you, but being examples to the flock'*

1 Peter 5:2-3

This often means identifying with people and not being aloof from them. Sometimes identification comes before impartation. I remember a pioneer missionary who had been ministering to a remote tribe telling me how he was sitting around the campfire with a group of leaders one night. Suddenly one of the leaders asked "Do white men cry? Do they know how to express their feelings and emotions?" "You have brought us medicine, roads, bridges, the gospel, but we still feel we do not know who you really are".

Good leaders will identify with people. They will not become a mystery. They will be open and honest. Not just sharing their victories but also their struggles. They will lead by example.

*'But be an **example** to the believers...do not neglect the gift that is in you...that your **progress** may be evident to all'.*

1 Timothy 4:12

## Good Leaders make Good Fathers

Good leaders are not dictators who want to Lord it over the flock. They usually have a great love and respect for those that are in their care. Paul said

*'But we were **gentle** among you...**affectionately** longing for you...we **exhorted** and **comforted** you and charged every one of you as a **father** does his children'.*

1 Thessalonians 2:7-11

A father is both loving and firm. He imparts security and warmth to the home, as do spiritual fathers to the church. My father was basically a good father although when I was growing up he was not a born-again Christian. He was both loving and firm. We went fishing and shooting together and we had a good relationship. The only exception was as a youngster I would be playing with the neighbourhood kids and had no idea of the time. My dad hated being late and if I was late home he would lose it and come after me and take his belt off to whack me all the way home if he could catch me.

We need more good spiritual fathers today. We have plenty of evangelists, teachers, and pastors but not a lot of really good fathers. This was also a problem in the early church.

> '... You may have ten thousand instructors in Christ yet you do not have many *fathers*'.
>
> 1 Corinthians 4:15

## Empowered for Ministry

Good men inspire and empower others for ministry. Jesus instructed His disciples to tarry in the city of Jerusalem until they were endued with power from on high (Luke 24:49).

I was at a Ministers leadership meeting recently. After the meeting I spoke to a young man who was pioneering a church and asked him how he enjoyed the meeting, he said, to be honest, he was very disappointed. Asking why he felt that way, he said he was hoping to be empowered for ministry. From his perspective, there was too much time spent on the administrative side of ministry, rather than the empowerment side of ministry. I assured him that the administrative side was necessary, but that I fully understood what he meant.

I remembered when I was younger how hungry I was to be empowered by the Holy Spirit for ministry. I would spend time worshiping and seeking the Lord in prayer. I would be hoping for a Prophesy and desiring the laying on of hands for an impartation. There was always an expectation to be empowered by the Holy Spirit.

It is one thing to be on a mission with a purpose. It is another thing to be equipped for that mission. Jesus made this clear when he said to His disciples.

> *'But you shall receive **power** when the*
> *Holy Spirit has come upon you;*

Acts 1:8

## Arthur Blessitt on Spiritual Development

Arthur carried a wooden cross around the world. One of the most inspiring men I have ever met.

I have transcribed most of this message that Arthur gave to Bible College Students.

I want to talk to you about spiritual development in leadership. I want to base what I have to say on Luke 21:25-26.

'And on the earth distress of nations...men's hearts failing them from *fear* and the expectation of those things which are coming upon the earth'.

I want to speak to you about fear because in the last days we will all be affected by fear.

Fear can make your study worthless, you may have all the answers, you may have a thorough knowledge of the Bible, you may have excelled in theology, you may be thoroughly trained, but if you are afraid, God will not be able to use you.

We all have a fear of failure - not just a fear of other people, but a fear of ourselves. We are afraid that we will fail. We are afraid that people will not listen to us.

We will fear the reactions of others, and as long as we dwell on reactions we will never go into action.

As Christians, we need to be free of fear. We should be able to stand straight, look people in the eye, there should be liberty in us, not fear.

Too many Christians live under the condemnation of the devil. They feel they are not worthy, that the Lord cannot use them. In Christ, we are new creatures. We are to walk not only in humility but also in dignity, as sons of God. The way you walk and talk and hold yourself is important. Your clothes may only be old rags, but it's the way you wear them that counts.

Most people fear death. I have faced death and lived through it, I have now been set free of the fear of death. If I fear death, I will have to run and keep running, and the devil would gain mastery over my life. But Jesus has destroyed the fear of death.

Many people are afraid of the future. They are afraid of making decisions. They really do not know where they are going. They lack direction and vision. You will never be a church leader if you are like that. You need to know the way. Jesus said, "I am the way". People like to follow a leader who knows the way.

Leaders need to be filled with Holy Spirit boldness. We need to be led by the Spirit, and have the fruit of the Spirit in our lives, to be able to reach others for Christ. As a leader, you must take the initiative. If you have to have someone push you all the time you will not make a good pastor or spiritual leader. It will be your zeal for God that will get the job done. Take a hold of God. Be like Jacob and take a hold of God for yourself.

# SECTION 3
## Opening up your Ministry

*'...and **Encourage them all**...'*

Acts 11:23

# Chapter 9
## Spreading the Gospel of the Kingdom

To unlock and expand our ministry we may need to to take a fresh look at our theology. I had someone ask me recently "How relevant is the Kingdom of God to our generation?" I believe it is very relevant because it gives people an alternative to this world system and should be a vital part of our ministry. The church has a responsibility to proclaim the gospel of the Kingdom. The apostle Paul spent a lot of time expounding the theology of the Kingdom of God.

*Then Paul dwelt two whole years in his own rented house, and received all who came to him, preaching the **kingdom of God** and **teaching** the things which concern the Lord Jesus Christ'.*

Acts 28:30-31

If we want to open up an area of our ministry we would do well to teach and preach more about the theology of the

Kingdom of God.

This is one of my favourite subjects. For my 'Bachelor of Ministry', I did a thesis on 'Missions and the Gospel of the Kingdom'.

## Church and Kingdom theology

The church is not to be confused with the Kingdom of God. The church is to proclaim the Gospel of the Kingdom. The 'Church' is from the Greek 'EKKLESIA' which means the 'called out ones'. Called out of the kingdom of darkness into the Kingdom of God to proclaim the Gospel of the Kingdom.

E. Stanley Jones says in his book 'The Unshakable Kingdom and the Unchanging Person'

> The Christian church while it holds within itself the best life of the kingdom, is not the kingdom of God. The kingdom is absolute, the church is relative- relative to something beyond itself, the kingdom. The church is not an end in itself, the kingdom is the end'.

On the other hand, the word 'Kingdom' throughout the New Testament comes from the Greek word 'BASILEIA'. It means a kingdom, a realm, a region that is governed by a king.

Graeme Goldsworthy in his book 'Gospel and Kingdom' puts it this way;

'We may best understand this concept in terms of the

relationship of a ruler to subjects. That is, there is a king who rules a people, and a sphere where this rule is recognized as taking place.

So the kingdom of God is basically coming under the rule of God. Through our Lord Jesus Christ.

## A time of discouragement

As much as I loved Lismore, and the church I was Pastoring, I still went through a time of discouragement. The church was not growing like I had expected. I complained to the Lord about the fact that it was a rural city and that we kept losing people to the capital cities. We seemed to no sooner gain some people only to lose others. The cycle seemed to be continuous.

It was as though the Lord asked me, "Where are they going, and what are they doing?" As far as I knew they were going to Brisbane, Sydney, Melbourne and other areas for work, or for their education. I also knew that most of them were settled into churches and many of them were serving the Lord in some capacity.

It was as though the Lord said very clearly to me "The church may not have grown, but my Kingdom has still grown as a result of your church".

That was enough to dispel my discouragement. I realized that there was a bigger picture that I was not seeing at the time. The Church expands the Kingdom of God. Even though it's nice to have a big church. The church has a purpose and that purpose is to proclaim and extend the kingdom.

So I encourage those who may be struggling with a similar problem to see the bigger picture.

## What is the substance of the Kingdom?

How can we best describe the kingdom? It appears to be nebulous and has no real substance. That is because it is spiritual, not literal.

> *'For the kingdom of God is not food and drink, but righteousness and peace and joy in the **Holy Spirit**'.*
>
> Romans 14:17

Jesus in answering the Pharisees question "When will the kingdom come?" By his answer, He was saying it is here now. A kingdom that is manifest within us. It has to be of a spiritual nature.

> *'...the kingdom of God does not come with observation; nor will they say "See here!" For indeed the kingdom of God is **within you**'.*
>
> Luke 17:20-21

There is, however, a more literal kingdom that is still yet to come. This kingdom is the eternal reign of God, ushered in at the return of Christ, a kingdom where Christ reigns throughout eternity.

Erich Sauer in his book 'From Eternity to Eternity' puts it

this way;

Salvation has arrived, and therefore the good news which Jesus proclaims describes a kingdom which had both already come and is yet coming'.

Yes, the Kingdom has a very real function and purpose as an alternative to this world system.

## Healing the sick

Preaching the gospel of the kingdom includes healing the sick. Jesus sent his disciples out and said to them.

> *'Preach the kingdom of God is at hand,* **heal the sick**... *Freely you have received, freely give'*
>
> Matthew 10:9-10

I have seen many sick people healed in Jesus name. I was ministering on the Island of Daru. It was an exciting time. I prayed for a man in a meeting who had been bowed over for years with a back condition. Nothing appeared to happen immediately so I went on praying for other people. Suddenly I heard a lot of shouting and clapping. I looked around to see this man walking around with a straight back. The next night most of the patients from the local hospital turned up for prayer. Many testified to being healed.

Allan Meyer and I were in charge of a healing meeting at LMC in Melbourne. A lady from a Catholic Church brought her 12-year-old son who had a brain tumour. The doctors had given him 3 months to live. We prayed for him. Three months later I had a phone call from the mother to say her son had been given a clean bill of health and was back at school living a normal life.

## What should we promote?

The Church or the Kingdom or both. One compliments the other, so we should promote both.

Jesus said repent for the kingdom is at hand. He did not say repent because religion is at hand, or the Temple is at hand, or the Scribes and Pharisees are at hand. In other words, His priority at the time was the proclamation of the kingdom. As good as our denomination maybe we should never lose sight of the gospel of the kingdom.

> '*This **gospel of the kingdom** must be preached in all the world as a witness'.*
>
> Matthew 24:14

## The keys to the kingdom

What are the keys to the kingdom? It would appear that Peter used those keys on the day of Pentecost when the Holy Spirit was poured out on the waiting disciples.

When the people heard Peter preach they were convicted and wanted to get right with God. They said to Peter "What shall we do? His answer was

> '***Repent*** *and let every one of you be **baptized** in the name of Jesus Christ for the remission of sins,*

*and you shall receive the **gift of the Holy Spirit**'.*

Acts 2:38

As a result, many turned to the Lord and these keys were put into action. I will expound them one at a time as follows.

**1. Repentance**

In answer to the question "What shall we do?" Peter said, "Repent". John the Baptist and Jesus had both introduced the Kingdom by saying "Repent". Repentance is turning away from sin and turning to God for His forgiveness.

**2. Water Baptism**

John the Baptist had spoken of Baptism as an act of repentance. "I indeed baptize you with water unto repentance"(Matthew 3:11). This is an outward act of an inner repentance, to signify publically a desire to follow Christ.

**3. The Baptism in the Holy Spirit**

Jesus spoke of the Baptism in the Holy Spirit. "He will baptize you with the Holy Spirit and fire" (Matthew 3:11) This was to empower the early church believers to be witnesses for Christ in a hostile world. (Acts 1:8)

The early Church went out using these keys as an introduction to enter the Kingdom. When I was first saved I was taught this was the pattern to follow. However, I was baptised in the Holy Spirit with the evidence of speaking in tongues sometime before I was baptised in water. These are basic steps, but we have to be careful not to restrict God to certain formulas.

# Chapter 10
## Helping to plant and establish Churches

Helping to plant and establish churches is another way of unlocking and opening up our ministry. Before we do anything, we need to assess if existing churches are having an impact in the area we are thinking of planting a church. If not, we may need to plant a church for likeminded believers to meet. It would become a base for them in the community for teaching, and evangelism. Our main concern and focus should be to spread the gospel.

The very first church was established in Jerusalem. However, the believers had become a little too comfortable. God had to use persecution to get the believers out of Jerusalem. This was so that they would scatter, and sow the seed of the word, through evangelism and planting churches.

## Seed is not for the Barn

Seed is not fruitful if it stays in the barn. Seed must be sown. So must the word of God. In Haggai 2:19 God asks the question.

*'Is the **seed** still in the **barn**?'*

God cannot bless seed that is still in the barn. The seed of the word needs to be scattered and sown in the field. This may result in a church plant.

## Sowing the seed of the Word

We have a responsibility to sow the seed of the word. We will often plant a church depending on the results of sowing that seed. We know that only a percentage of what we sow will take root and become fruitful. Jesus said in the parable;

*'Behold a **sower** went out to sow'*

Matthew 13:3

To sow seed we have to get out of the church and evangelize and witness. In the parable, Jesus explains that some seed fell by the wayside, some on stony places, and some among thorns. These seeds never survived. So we know for whatever reason we will not always have success. However, some fell on good ground and yielded a harvest. The seed that falls on good ground is usually the best place to plant a church. Often in cases like this, a group of people will come together in an area to form the foundation of a church plant.

## Getting something started

A church plant may begin with a prayer meeting or a home group that eventually develops into a church plant. Usually, an appointed person will initially be sent from the home church to oversee the church. Then in time, they will appoint elders. We see that Paul selects Titus for a similar task.

*'For this reason, I left you in Crete, that you should **set in order** the things that are lacking, and **appoint elders** in every city as I commanded you'.*

Titus 1:5

When I was in Melbourne I was asked if I would be willing to start a church plant in the town of Healesville. The Melbourne youth group took three outreach meetings in Healesville and had made seven contacts. I was given seven names on a piece of paper with their phone numbers. That is all I had at the time. We followed up the contacts and initially started with a prayer meeting. This grew into a church meeting in a public hall. A little over a year later we had about 30 regulars and appointed someone else to lead it.

Arthur F. Glasser in his book 'Kingdom and Mission' encourages the planting of churches.

'The Christian movement needs even more than strongly committed individuals. It needs Christians gathering together in strong churches. The missionary task is incomplete if it stops short of planting churches'.

**Laying a foundation for a church** (Acts 2:44-47). The early church laid the following foundation-

1. Apostles Doctrine (Sound Teaching).

2. Fellowship (Believers Meeting Together).

3. Breaking of Bread (Communion).

4. Prayer and Praise (Worship).

5. Sharing (Meeting the Needs of the Needy)

6. Wonders and Signs (Healings)

7. Those added to the Church (New Converts)

## Teaching the First Principles and more

A good church foundation will also need to have good teaching. The basics need to be taught, such the 'elementary principles' as mentioned in Hebrews 6:1-2. They are listed as -

1. Repentance from dead works.

2. Faith toward God.

3. The doctrine of Baptisms.

4. Laying on of hands.

5. The resurrection of the dead.

6. Eternal Judgment.

However, the writer of Hebrews encourages believers to move on from these principles. He calls them the milk of the word. He would rather have them move on to the meat of the word, and not be just continually going over these basics (Hebrews 5:12-14). What does he mean by the meat of the word? He mentions moving on to 'perfection' or maturity. Other sections in the book of Hebrews, give us insight into understanding what he may refer to as the meat of the word.

He deals with the fact that Christ and the new covenant are superior to the Judaic system. He highlights the 'better' things the new covenant has to offer as a result of Christ. It is based on better promises, better than the law, a better priesthood, better sacrifices, better possessions, a better country, a better resurrection. He expounds the scriptures to show that there is more to be gained by being in Christ and a part of the New Covenant.

## Our greatest gift is Love

A church plant can have a foundation like the early church, all the basic doctrines, all the gifts of the Spirit, but if it has no love it is of no profit. 1 Corinthians 13 is all about love, and it is placed in between chapters 12 and 14 that deal with the operation of prophecy and spiritual gifts, including speaking in tongues. When it comes to church life our greatest gift is love.

*And now abide faith, hope, love, these three;*
*but the **greatest of these is love**'.*

Hebrews 13:13

Firstly, why is love so important? We read in 13:8 that 'Love never fails'. The gifts may fail but not love. Love is an everlasting quality, for God is love.

Secondly, what does love look like? We have a list in 13: 4-7 where we read, it is patient, kind, not envious, not puffed up with pride, is not rude, not selfish, not easily provoked, thinks no evil, rejoices in truth, bears all things, believes all things, endures all things. It sure looks like perfection.

Thirdly, Jesus commanded His disciples to love one another. In John 13 34-35 we read 'By this (love) all will know that you are my disciples if you have a love for one another'. So the greatest gift a church plant has in the community is Love.

## The lost need to be saved

This is not going to happen unless we are prepared to evangelise. We may not all be called to be evangelists. But we are called to sow our seed and be witnesses for Christ. It may be among family and friends, it could be our neighbours, or in the workplace. It may be to complete strangers as the opportunity arises. Jesus came to save the lost.

*'For the son of man has come to **save** that which was **lost'**.*

Matthew 18:11

## The impact of an Evangelistic ministry

It was Philip the evangelist that went down to the city of Samaria. He preached Christ and miracles were in abundance.

He was experiencing a revival. We read in Acts 8:5-8.

> '*Philip went down to the city of Samaria and preached* **Christ** *to them. And multitudes with one accord heeded the things spoken by Philip, hearing and seeing the* **miracles** *which he did'.*

This was a great testimony to the risen Lord. It was demonstrating that Jesus was alive and confirming the word being preached, with signs, wonders, and miracles. Jesus can do the same today.

> '*Jesus Christ the* **same**, *yesterday, today, and forever'.*
>
> *Hebrews 13:8*

Vince Esterman has impacted many with his evangelistic ministry and pioneering spirit. He and his wife Denise pioneered a church in Ipswich. Vince speaks French fluently so they went to Paris and pioneered churches in France. I saw Vince in action on the streets of Paris preaching with his sketch board. I was amazed at his boldness and ability to draw a crowd. At the time of writing, they are pioneering churches on Reunion Island.

## Jesus' expectation of the Church

Jesus expected the church to proclaim the gospel of the kingdom throughout the world. This would have been impossible with limited resources to accomplish in the days of Jesus.

> '*Go into* **all the world and preach the gospel** *to every creature'.*

Mark 16:15

We can only assume that this expectation was to be transferred to all disciples of all generations, through the Church age, to be fulfilled before the end comes. Jesus Himself confirms this by stating

> '...*this gospel of the kingdom will be preached in all the world as a witness to all nations,* **and then the end will come**'.

Matthew 24:14

The gospel must be presented as an alternative to this unstable world system. People are looking for something more today. Unfortunately, sometimes they seek out other substitutes instead of the kingdom of God. But the Church holds the answers.

Dr Lester Sumrall in his book 'The Gifts and Ministry of the Holy Spirit' puts it this way

> 'The infant church born in Jerusalem, went forth to challenge and defy the entire Roman Empire with all its paganism, sensualism, witchcraft, and military might. Rome fell but the church marches on'.

## Planting Churches in PNG

While we were on the mission field in PNG we were in revival and there were churches being planted at a rapid rate throughout the nation. When we first arrived there were around 35 churches relating to our movement. By the time we left six years later, there were around 75. This was due to national leaders like Bob Lutu, Charles Lapa, Pinaria Sialis, Lenden Butuna, and a host of others who were prepared to go or send out others. Many miracles accompanied the preaching of the word.

## Church Planting back in Australia

Apart from those already mentioned. Our church in Lismore NSW was instrumental in planting churches in Kyogle and Yamba. We were able to get Barry and Joan Winton who were missionaries in Bougainville to come and establish the church in Kyogle. At the time of writing it is now being led by James and Danielle Howes. Chris Maynard came down from the Gold Coast to establish the Yamba church after we had laid the foundation.

Both of these church plants were a result of myself and Rod Dymock my associate, and others, being rostered on to hold prayer meetings, and Sunday meetings in both places before they became established churches with designated leaders. This stretched our time and our resources, but the end result was two well-established churches.

**UNLOCKING** Your **PURPOSE**

# Chapter 11
## Considering the Culture

Considering the Culture where we minister will help to unlock and open up our ministry. The word culture can be interpreted and applied in different ways. A Football Coach may want to change the culture of the players and the Club. A Manager, the culture of the employees and the Business. A Pastor, the culture of the elders and the Church. This is usually the process of changing old methods and ways of doing things, to new ways and methods. It is introducing new thinking and taking steps that will help turn things around. Traditionally, culture refers to different people groups, which we will address.

It was in Antioch that the disciples were first called 'Christians'. Regardless of their background and culture, it would appear that this then became the most accepted term for the Disciples and followers of Christ. As Christians they were relatively free of their own culture and traditions, to pursue the cause of Christ, and proclaim the gospel.

Communication is vital if the gospel is going to have an impact and be able to reach many different people groups.

## Finding Common Ground

One of the keys to expressing the gospel in a Multi-Cultural environment is to find common ground. The word for communication is derived from the Latin word 'COMMUNIS' which means common. There are a number of scriptural examples –

Jesus said to Simon Peter and his brother Andrew who were professional fishermen;

*'Follow me and I will make you **fishers** (common ground) of men'.*

Jesus to the Samaritan women at the well asks her for a drink from the well. In the course of this dialogue, Jesus skilfully makes his point;

*"Whoever drinks of **this water** (common ground) will thirst again. But whoever drinks of the water that I shall give him will never thirst".*

John 4:13-14

Paul in Athens came across people worshipping idols. One of the objects being worshipped had an inscription 'To the unknown God'. His response was;

*'I perceive that in all things you are **very religious***'
*(common ground) 'Therefore the one whom you worship without knowing, Him I proclaim to you'*

Acts 17:22-23

Whether we are preaching, teaching, or witnessing we need to be sensitive to seize on areas of common ground to communicate the gospel.

## Adjusting to a Multi-Cultural environment

Many nations today, including Australia, have become multi-cultural. In Australia, we also need to consider and respect our indigenous culture. Therefore we need to be wise enough to make some adjustments at times. We want to be able to communicate with these different people groups. This is an essential communicative skill that we need to consider, study, develop and apply. It is something we have to keep working on to effectively communicate the gospel.

David J Hesselgrave in the preface to his book 'Communicating Christ Cross-Culturally says

'…communication is the name of the game, our special task is to cross over cultural and other boundaries in order to communicate Christ'.

How skilled are we at performing this important task? Can we make adjustments without compromising the gospel? As Christians, we have a common purpose despite cultural differences. We are to present the gospel in an acceptable manner.

Pius Wakatama in his book 'Independence for the third world church' says;

'If Christ cannot penetrate cultures then we had better stop singing "There is power in the blood".

## The flexibility of the Apostle Paul

The apostle Paul was the master of communication when it came to identifying with other cultures and people groups. He fully understood the value of Cross-Cultural differences to spread the gospel.

> ' For though I am free from all men, I have made myself a servant to all, that I might win the more; and to the Jews, I became as a **Jew** that I might win Jews; to those who are under the **law**, as under the law, that I might win those who are under the law; to those who are without law, as **without law** (not being without the law toward God, but under law toward Christ), that I might win those who are without the law; to the weak I became as **weak**, that I might win the weak; I have become **all things** to all men, that I might, by all means, save some.
>
> 1 Corinthians 9:19-23.

This is a classic example of flexibility in every situation. It is still the same gospel, but presented with skill and understanding, when facing the many cultural differences that existed.

Kenneth Burke expresses this comprehensively in his book 'A Rhetoric of Motives';

'You persuade a man in so far as you can talk his language by speech, gesture, tonality, order, image, attitude, idea, identifying your ways with his'.

## The cultural setting of the 'Peace Child' story

When Don Richardson confronted the Sawi people with the gospel he ran into a major problem. The hero to the gospel story was Judas because of the value the Sawi placed on deception, treachery, and betrayal.

If it had not been for him stumbling across their traditional culture that accepted a 'Peace Child', they would have somehow managed to slot Jesus into their own pagan mythology.

He discovered that warring tribes could stop the war, and return to a peaceful existence with one another if one of the warring tribes were to give up one of their babies as a 'Peace Child' to appease the other tribe.

Don saw how he could get the true gospel message across to the Sawi. He began to proclaim that Jesus came as a 'Peace Child'. The people saw the parallel and immediately responded and accepted Christ as their one and only 'Peace Child'.

So here we see that culture instead of being a stumbling block became a catalyst for the proclamation of the gospel.

May God grant us such wisdom to use culture to advance the spread of the gospel of the kingdom.

## Try and avoid misunderstandings

We also need to be aware that some cultural differences are sensitive issues that we need to respect to avoid misunderstandings. I was preaching to a remote tribe through an interpreter and I used the phrase "We shouldn't throw the baby out with the bathwater". Well, this caused an uproar among the people. They took it literally and were horrified to think that someone would do such a terrible thing.

## Using some license to explain scripture

In chapter one, I mentioned among the shark hunters of Kontu that I said 'the devil was like a savage shark' instead of 'like a roaring lion' as they could relate to sharks, not lions. I heard a young national man pray around the communion table "Lord take away our sins and make us white like the inside of a coconut". Instead of quoting the scripture "as white as snow" as it didn't snow in these tropical areas.

## Identifying with those we minister to

Sometimes it is hard for people to identify with leaders. They are perceived as being so superior. We need to reassure our hearers that we too are mere mortals saved by grace. When Paul and Barnabas were being idolized on one occasion they tore their clothes and ran through the crowd saying

*'We also are men with the **same nature** as you'*

Acts 14:15

## A reason for National Identity

In these days we see more and more nations are gaining their independence from nations with different cultures. Could there be a purpose to this? I believe so. For the scripture says that it is God that establishes the boundaries of the nations.

*'...and He has made from one blood every nation...and has appointed their pre-appointed times and the boundaries of their habitation, so that they should **seek** the Lord'.*

Acts 17:26-27

The reason is that the Lord desires that nations' should seek Him. It appears that the Lord will give nations their independence, to give them the opportunity to seek Him, without perhaps the outside influences of other cultures.

Does this mean that there will be no need for cross-cultural ministry? No not at all, because most nations are already very multi-cultural. This includes linguistic, social, economic, religious, racial, political, traditional, and other customary differences.

So culture should be considered. Yes, but not so much that it becomes a hindrance to the spread of the gospel.

**UNLOCKING** Your **PURPOSE**

# Chapter 12
## A Home Base and Spiritual Warfare

To spread the gospel, a Home Base and Spiritual Warfare will help us accomplish much more than if we were to remain independent. It will unlock much-needed resources and prayer support.

The church at Jerusalem became the very first home base. It did not remain independent it was involved with outreach and helping others to become established.

> *'Then news of these things came to the ears of the church in **Jerusalem**, and they **sent** out Barnabas to go as far as Antioch.'*
>
> Acts 11:22

The church in Jerusalem took on the responsibility of sending out ministry. We see this principle earlier in the book of Acts as to what seemed to be a repetitive pattern that they followed.

> *'Now when the apostles who were at **Jerusalem** heard that Samaria had received the word of God, they **sent** Peter and John to them'.*
>
> Acts 8:14

This is the Apostolic ministry in action. A little later in Acts 13 the church at Antioch also became a home base, like the church in Jerusalem. They sent out Barnabas and Saul (Paul) on other missions.

However, when a major dispute arose they took it back to the home base in Jerusalem (Acts 15:2).

## Supply from a Home Base

We were so grateful to have had a home base support us while we were on the mission field. Without this source of supply, we would never have survived. We were supported with a small income as well as school fees for our children to attend international schools in Port Moresby.

We never took anything from the local people. The church offerings paid church expenses and wages for the national pastors. We also received large amounts from Australia to extend the Church, Bible College, and other buildings, including some maintenance.

## Praying for extra provisions

When we are serving the Lord with a Purpose He is faithful to supply for our needs. God provides in strange ways, sometimes through complete strangers. Usually, he supplies through those we are connected to in some way.

At times we would run short of money because of extra unforeseen expenses. God was faithful to provide just what we needed at the right time. There was one little old widow lady from our Home Base that was obviously hearing from God. She would often send us small amounts at the right time to meet a particular need.

## The Benefits of a Home Base

Any form of outreach will always benefit by being closely connected to a home base. There are many benefits to having a home base. One has already been mentioned. The sorting out of disputes or doctrinal differences that may arise. A good home base will offer prayer support. Also, ministry to help in times of need. Including wisdom from often more experienced ministry.

Home bases usually prefer churches to be autonomous, but they can be a source of supply and financial help to get the church started. We will always serve God and pursue our calling more effectively by being connected to a home base.

## A Principle of War

A Home base is a principle of war. The first thing an army seeks to do is establish a home base. The base is essential to keep the supplies up to the troops on the front line. It is also a place where battle-weary troops can retreat to rest and be replenished.

Abram (Abraham) applied principles of war.

> 'he armed his three hundred and eighteen **trained servants**...*who went in pursuit*... **dividing forces** *by night he attacked them*...*so he* **brought back** *his brother Lot and his goods*...'
>
> Genesis 14:12-16

Abram applied these principles of war –

1. He had a **home base** to **train** men

2. He went into **action** with a **definite plan**

3. He had a **purpose** (to bring Lot back)

These are basic principles of war that all began from having a home base to train people.

## Unity in battle a real key

Another important key to the battlefield is unity.

> 'Who went out to battle, expert in war with all weapons of war, stouthearted, men who could **keep rank**'.
>
> 1 Chronicles 12:33

This is a picture of not only skilled men in war but also ones who could keep rank. They were disciplined. The devil knows how important this principle is. He knows a divided kingdom cannot stand in battle. When Jesus was accused of casting out demons by the power of 'Beelzebub' the ruler of demons he said

*'If Satan casts out Satan, he is **divided** against himself. How then will his kingdom stand?'*

Matthew 12:26

A missionary from Africa shared how he was sitting on the veranda one-night watching Gecko's feeding on insects attracted to a light. Suddenly one Gecko attacked another Gecko and the insects escaped. The Lord said to him "When churches fight amongst themselves the harvest escapes".

## Prayer and spiritual warfare

When I was an assistant pastor in Melbourne I was put in charge of a Spiritual Warfare meeting together with Jill Oxley who was a real prayer warrior. The main purpose of the meeting was to pray for the nation.

I struggled with this concept until I had a dream. I dreamt I was the personal bodyguard to the Prime Minister. I was sleeping in a guard house at the Prime Minister's residence. In this dream, a squadron of black objects started to fly over. Then suddenly two of them spotted me and came through the window to attack me. I grabbed my revolver and started shooting at them. It made no difference. Then I yelled out the name "Jesus". They immediately disappeared.

Shaken by the dream the Lord led me to read 2 Corinthians 10:3-4

> '...we do not war according to the flesh. For the **weapons** of our warfare are **not carnal** but **mighty in God** for the pulling down of **strongholds.**'

I learned several things through this experience -

1. The enemy is real and attacks nations.

2. Our weapons are not carnal but spiritual.

3. The name of 'Jesus' is so powerful.

4. Attacks can be repelled through prayer.

## Know your Enemy

Another important principle of war is to know something about your enemy. We all know that the devil is our real enemy. He is a liar and the master of deception. He will often try and hinder our progress. Paul says;

> '...we wanted to come to you-even I, Paul, time and again-but **Satan hindered us**'.
>
> 1 Thessalonians 2:18

The Greek word for hindered is 'egkopto' which means to 'cut into', 'impede', 'detain'. He will throw a spanner in the works to mess things up to stop us from fulfilling our destiny. However, God is still in control.

I was ministering in the beautiful 'Duke of York Islands' where we were preaching and showing a movie and having an incredible response. I had to get back to Rabaul on a Friday to catch a plane to Kavieng to take a wedding on Saturday. I missed the boat which had left at 2 am instead of 4 am. There was no communication in those days and I was upset and walking along the beach trying to figure out how to get to Rabaul. Two men in a canoe paddled over to me from a nearby island and asked if we could come that night to preach and show the movie on their island. I said we would. It was a great night, people ran forward to receive Christ many were healed and delivered. I was able to get a boat ride back to Rabaul the next day, but I did not arrive in Kavieng until Sunday. Thinking I had missed the wedding I started to apologize when I was met at the airport. They said "No problem we had decided to put the wedding off until today, Sunday, so you are still in time to take it". God had it all under control.

What are we up against personally? How is he likely to attack us, or our church? Jesus gives us some insight.

*'First bind the **strongman**'.*

Matthew 12:29

There appears to be strong men and strongholds in the realm of the Spirit that need to be bound through prayer. They may be over cities or regions it's good to try and discern who or what we are up against.

For example in PNG, Sorcery and Witchcraft were obvious

because of traditions and culture.

A young missionary told me how he was sent into a remote area in the mountainous Highlands of PNG. He awoke one night to find a demon manifesting beside his bed. It looked like a very old man with dreadlocks. It pointed at him and said, "Leave this area because these people are mine, they have belonged to me for centuries". The young missionary said, "No, you are wrong they belong to Christ, they have been redeemed by the Blood, You must leave". Shortly after that encounter revival broke out. There were manifestations of angels. Many turned to Christ.

## An Article in the Brisbane Courier-Mail

Here is an extract from an article written in The Brisbane Courier-Mail printed on 6th October 2018.

> 'The number of people falling victim to sorcery-related violence and killings are on the rise in PNG. A new study from Oxfam, in partnership with Q.U.T., reveals that there were 232 reported cases of sorcery-related violence. Experts warn that this is only the tip of the iceberg. There is an upsurge in witchcraft-related violence.

## In Australia

It seems to be much harder to know what we are up against in Australia. If we consider our culture of 'She'll be right Mate' we could be dealing with apathy, laziness, unbelief, tradition, religion. On the other hand, our Ned Kelly attitude of 'Such is life' could indicate lawlessness, violence, anger, hate, lies, and so on.

I was ministering in a public hall in country Victoria and a lady started to manifest. She kept shouting "Help is on the way". "Help is on the way". Suddenly two members of a Cult (I will not mention which one) burst in saying "What's happening in here?" I felt at the time that this would have indicated a spirit of 'Religion' over that area.

I would encourage Christians to stay connected to a home base, and not to be afraid at times, to engage in Spiritual Warfare.

### Dealing with demons

Sometimes demons can be responsible for all kinds of bondage. Habits that cannot be broken, addictions, tormenting mental disorders, some fears, sicknesses, and diseases.

Demons need to be cast out at times. But we need discernment. Deliverance is no substitute for self-discipline, and obedience to God. Demons hate the truth. I was in a meeting preaching and a lady interrupted me and said "I hate your preaching I can't stand your preaching" I was quite offended and demanded to know why. Still manifesting and holding her hands over her ears she yelled: "Too much truth I can't stand the truth". Jesus said;

*'You shall know the truth and the **truth** will make you free".*

John 8:32

Start talking about the cross and the blood of Christ and who we are in Christ. Exalt the name of Jesus. The demons hate it. They know they have no answer to the redemptive work of Christ.

A part of our purpose in ministry is to set people free, that they might be healed and able to serve the Lord with great joy and freedom.

*'For this **purpose** was the Son of God manifested, that He might destroy the works of the devil'.*

1 John 3:8

In Port Moresby, we ran a Tuesday night Bible School that attracted some prominent expatriates, like missionary Maria Von Trapp (one of the actual children portrayed in the movie 'Sound of Music'). One night a lady with a Catholic background stayed behind to tell me that her marriage was in trouble and she was about to leave her husband and take her three children back to Australia. Her husband was an officer in the Australian Navy and had been posted to Port Moresby. She told me he had a drinking problem and that she could not handle it any longer. I told her to try and get him to come and see me.

There was a knock on the door about 8 am the next morning. When I opened the door there was a man standing there in a Navy uniform. He told me that his wife said that I might be able to help him. I invited him in and asked him to explain his situation. The bottom line was that he wanted to save his marriage. I told him that he needed to be saved first and led him in a Sinner's prayer. I then said let's pray about this alcohol problem. I commanded the spirit of alcohol to leave him. He was thrown on the floor and got up a new man.

A few weeks later I looked around in our Sunday morning service and saw this man with his wife and family all worshipping the Lord. She never did leave. When he eventually returned to Australia he left the Navy and managed several Christian Bookshops.

## Using Prophetic Words to wage War

Paul encouraged Timothy to use prophetic words over his life to wage a good warfare.

> '*This charge I commit to you, son Timothy, according to the* **prophecies** *previously made concerning you, that* **by them** *you may* **wage the good warfare**...'
>
> 1 Timothy 1:18

I have used personal prophecies over my life to wage war against the enemy when I have felt that I have been under attack and that the enemy is trying to undermine my faith. I have drawn aside in prayer with some prophecies that I have had written down. When you have been given a personal prophecy, if it has been recorded, get a copy of it, or write down what you remember for future use against the enemy. It will strengthen your faith and help you to stand your ground, resist the devil, and overcome whatever you face.

**UNLOCKING Your PURPOSE**

# Chapter 13
## The Purpose of Provision and Prosperity

To unlock and pursue our God-given purpose we will need to experience provision and prosperity. At times, that may need to be self-generating. Some ministers in smaller churches today have full or part-time jobs until the church is able to support them. Paul at times in his ministry worked for wages to make ends meet.

> '...he was of the **same trade**, he stayed with them and **worked**'. Acts 18:3

> 'I have coveted no one's silver or gold or apparel... **these hands have provided** for my necessities and for those who were with me'.
>
> Acts 20:33-34

Paul did not want to be a financial burden to anyone. However, there are other references where he thanks other believers and churches for providing for him.

> '...you **sent aid** once and again for my **necessities**'.
>
> Philippians 4:16

## How to Prosper for a Purpose

What is the key to prosperity?

If you are reading this you are probably hoping I can give you a quick fix so that you become prosperous. However, biblical prosperity is usually a process. A combination of divine principles over a period of time.

Prosperity is nearly always conditional. For example, Joshua was told if he meditated upon the word, confessed it, obey it, and applied it he would have good success.

> '...For **then** you will make your way **prosperous**, and then you will have good success'.
>
> Joshua 1:9

We will all go through trials and our faith will be tested. But we should still expect good success.

Again we read in the scriptures -

> 'Beloved I pray that you may prosper in all things and be in health, just as your **soul prospers**'.
>
> 3 John 2

There may be various ways of interpreting prosperity. It can mean different things to different people. I think the bottom line is that we have a relatively successful journey through life. We prosper to be in a position to give by sharing our prosperity with others.

## Give generously

God would have us to be generous in our giving. In fact, the scripture implies that the more generous we become the more we will prosper. Paul said;

*'He who **sows** sparingly will also reap sparingly, and he who **sows** bountifully will also reap bountifully'.*

2 Corinthians 9:6

The purpose behind this is to enable us to have more than enough so that we can share and help others who may be in need.

*'...then the disciples each **according to his ability**, determined to **send relief** to the brethren dwelling in Judea'.*

Acts 11:29

## Do not neglect your own family

It can be a trap to become so engrossed in ministry that we neglect our own family. We all have a responsibility to provide for our own family.

*'But if anyone does not **provide** for his own, and especially for*

> *those of **his household**, he has denied the faith and is worse than an unbeliever'.*
>
> 1 Timothy 5:8

For example, we have a responsibility to work for an income. We need to provide finances for food, clothing, rent, or a mortgage, transport, and other basic needs. This can often be a challenge. Most of us will have to take out a mortgage if we want to own our own home. But we need to make sure we can cover the repayments on any loan that we may have to repay.

## Some helpful Biblical principles

I will briefly outline some principles that have helped us in our ministry and marriage to prosper.

1. **Working for an income** – We need to work to earn an income. There is nothing like a steady wage to help us manage our finances.

2. **Saving for the Future** – We do not know what the future holds. So we need to build a reserve to cover future costs.

3. **Investing what you can** – If you can invest in something like Real Estate, Blue Chip Shares, Bank Bonds, Superannuation or other things that are reasonably secure I suggest you do so.

4. **Giving as a principle of Sowing** - We need to be generous in our giving. For the way we sow will also be the way we reap.

**5. Supporting a local Church** - We need to be supportive of a local church. Usually where we fellowship on a regular basis.

## Is it okay to make a profit?

I have come across a few Christians that feel guilty if they make a profit and prosper. However, it is a sound biblical principle to make a profit. For example, if you buy a house you expect to make a profit in Australia if you wait several years before selling. This is what business is all about. It's all about making a profit. That profit can be used to clear your debts or you can sow it back into making more profit that you might be blessed and a blessing.

We see this profit-making principle in the story of the widow woman in 2 Kings 4:1-7. She had lost her husband and was in debt. The creditors were knocking on the door. What was she to do? She sought help from the man of God. She gave him the only jar of oil that she had and borrowed lots of empty jars from her neighbours. The man of God performed a miracle and filled all the jars with oil from her one bottle of oil. Then he instructed her to go and sell the oil for a PROFIT and pay her debts with the profit she made.

She would have also had plenty of oil left over to sustain her for years to come.

Sometimes we have to invest what we have to make a profit. It is then the blessing of the Lord upon that investment that gives us prosperity.

For example, we received a small inheritance enough for a new car. We resisted that temptation and used it for a deposit on an investment house. That was the beginning of a small real estate investment portfolio. The Lord has blessed this, and it is now helping us in our retirement.

# SECTION 4

Opening up your Future

'...*they should* **continue** *with the Lord.*'

Acts 11:23

# Chapter 14
## What does the Future look like?

We live in a rapidly changing world that appears to undermine the values of Christianity. We already face a barrage of questionable changes as to just what is politically correct and acceptable today. The way things are going from a secular point of view we could ask 'Does the future even have a church?' The future is always unpredictable. However, one thing is for sure, the church is here to stay. What then is our future and where do we fit in? To answer this, we need to ask another question.

What is the future of the mainstream traditional denominations today? Statistics reveal that many of these churches are in decline. The ones that appear to be still growing, are those that are open to the Charismatic movement which has spread across many of the traditional churches.

The Pentecostal movement is still growing throughout

the world especially in third world countries. Despite splinter groups in both the Charismatic and Pentecostal movements, and some that are a way off track, these movements are the ones that are attracting more and more believers.

Perhaps we should be praying, as Pope John XXIII did, for a new 'Pentecost'.

If we believe the church has answers, and that the power of the Holy Spirit can change institutions, as well as individual lives, let us continue to pray until we will see communities and nations impacted by a fresh outpouring of the Holy Spirit.

However, in times of uncertainty, what is the future of ministering locally and overseas especially for missions and missionaries?

We live in a changing world. Nations are striving to gain their independence. Colonialism has given way to Nationalism. However, with Nations gaining their independence, a new set of problems have begun to emerge. The political climate is often unpredictable. Military 'coup de tat' can determine national leadership. In some parts of the world, governments can rise and fall almost overnight. The economy is often unstable.

Missions and Missionaries can no longer rely on the security of their colonial authorities.

Passport and Visa requirements can suddenly change. We cannot predict the future.

But none of this negates the need for Missions and Missionaries. This is all a part of fulfilling the great commission of Christ, despite the difficulties and the opposition we may face. Our purpose is to still spread the gospel of the kingdom.

## Conversions and Discipleship

The great commission is all about making disciples which is often a process that combines evangelism and teaching. It is a process over a period of time.

Alan R. Tippett in his book 'Verdict Theology in Missionary Theory' lists five stages to the conversion and discipleship process.

1. **Discovery** (Discovering Christ)

2. **Deliberation** (Forsaking to Follow)

3. **Determination** (Decision to Follow)

4. **Dissonance** (Difficulties cause Doubts)

5. **Discipline** (Submission to Christ)

The Missionary can never over emphasize the need for evangelism and conversions. Earl Stanley Jones who spent sixty years in India in his book 'Conversion' says

> 'Jesus divided humanity into two classes – the unconverted and the converted, the once born and the twice born. All men live on one side or the other side of that line. It is a division that runs through time and eternity'

I once had a neighbour say to me with some disdain that some 'Born Again Christians' tried to convert him to Christianity. Unfortunately, he was happy to stay among the unconverted, the 'once- born', and had no intention of turning to Christ. He is no longer our neighbour, but I still pray for him that one day he will join the 'twice-born'.

## The sent Ones

Those involved in outreach are sent ones. They are sent out from their home bases into other areas to proclaim the gospel. This is still necessary if people are to hear the gospel.

> *'How shall they call on Him in whom they have not believed? And how shall they believe in Him of whom they have not heard? And how shall they hear without a **preacher**? And how shall they preach unless they are **sent**'.*
>
> Romans 10:14-15

When we were sent out as missionaries, people reacted in two ways. Firstly, on the home front, people said: "Why not leave them alone, they are happy in their tropical paradise, God can speak to them without you going". Secondly, on the mission field in some areas we and other missionaries were greeted with "Why didn't you come sooner". The gospel is like a great light being turned on in areas of spiritual darkness.

Before the first Missionaries were sent to the Pacific Islands the people were in darkness and bound by ungodly practices including cannibalism. When Jesus came to this world the scripture describes it this way.

> *'The people who sat in **darkness** have seen a great **light**,
> and for those who sat in the region and shadow of
> death Light has dawned'.*
>
> Matthew 4:16

## The Coming of the Light

We were visiting Thursday Island in the Torres Strait. We were there at the time of 'The Coming of the Light Festival'. This is celebrated on July 1st every year. This festival is to celebrate the coming of the first missionary. In 1871 The London Missionary Society sent out Samuel McFarlane as a missionary to the Torres Strait Islands to convert the heathen. The Islands were at war with one another and practicing cannibalism. To his surprise, the people readily received the gospel. This brought peace and completely changed the whole region. They still celebrate this today calling it 'The coming of the light Festival'.

When you hear of incredible stories like this you can't help but be inspired and supportive of missions and missionaries. This demonstrates how the impact of missions can affect many generations to come.

After all, God has promised to pour out His Spirit upon all flesh in these last days

> *'And it shall come to pass in the **last days**, says God;
> That I will pour out **My Spirit on all flesh**'.*
>
> Acts 2:17

So we need to make the most of our time. May we seize the opportunities we have to spread the gospel. Churches still need to foster a zeal for outreach and missions and missionaries in particular.

## Working together for the same objective

When it comes to outreach, there is a great need for Churches and Missions to work together in harmony and unity to be successful.

*'I planted, Apollos watered*, but God gave the increase'.

1 Corinthians 3:6

Paul planted, Apollos watered. Some will plant others will water what has been planted. But it is God that gives the increase. Different ministries at different times will contribute in different ways. The church where we were based in Port Moresby was originally pioneered by a group of young people from 'YWAM'. John Pasterkamp became the founder and leader of that original church and the pioneer of the movement that was to follow.

Some years ago I was able to lead a young man to the Lord who was brought to me by his sister Pam, he was addicted to drugs. His name was Neil Meyer (younger brother of Allan Meyer). Neil became a great leader and now heads up 'Teen Challenge' in Victoria.

Our daughter Amanda Butel and her husband Carl, (who were instrumental in bringing this book together) have over the years had three terms ministering in Thailand with their family helping 'Destiny Rescue'. This organisation rescues mainly young girls out of the prostitution trade.

There are also many other Para-Church groups such as Prison Fellowships, City Missions, Food Banks, Soup Kitchens, Bible Translators, The Bible Society, The Gideon's, and a host of others.

**A sensitivity to those we desire to reach**

When it comes to the future we need a sensitivity to those we are trying to reach. I have sensed some ungracious attitudes towards nationals from many missionaries. If missionaries continue to be insensitive and assume that the national church needs constant supervision, they have insulted the capabilities of the national leaders.

I had one missionary say to me "The nationals can't do without me, the only way they will get rid of me is in a box". Well, that did not happen, but a few years later, the nationals rose up against his overbearing ways, and he needed to leave the country. A mission or missionary should continue to promote confidence, not control. They can do this by drawing alongside national leaders giving them support and encouragement. They can teach them and release them to manage their own Churches. Therefore to some extent, our future possibilities in outreach and missions may rest in our hands.

**The spoken word is still persuasive**

There is nothing like the personal touch. Sharing our personal testimony always has an impact. The word for 'persuade' is derived from the Greek 'Peitho' which is to convince. King Agrippa responds to Paul's testimony by saying 'You almost persuade me to become a Christian'. (Acts 26:28). Our mission is to 'persuade' as many as possible to become Christians.

## Some predictions about the future church

It is hard to make predictions about the future of the church because every generation is different. There are some things we should consider from a biblical perspective.

1. **The church is here to stay** (Matthew 16:18). Jesus said He will build His church and the gates of hell will not prevail against it.

2. **The church will increase** (Matthew 16:19). The church holds the keys of the kingdom and the gospel of the kingdom will be preached in all the world.

3. **The great commission** (Matthew 28:19). There is a need to hold to the mission and not just the church model of doing things to survive.

4. **The church gathering** (Hebrews 10:25). Assembling together will never be replaced by social media or 'just Jesus and me' individuals.

5. **The Body of Christ** (1 Corinthians 12:12). The church is made up of many members all with different functions. People engaging will drive attendance.

All churches have a place, large or small, size may be irrelevant to the effectiveness of a church.

# Chapter 15

## Understanding Times and Seasons

To be effective in the future at pursuing our God-given purpose we will need to have a good understanding of times and seasons.

Saul and Barnabas taught for a season in Antioch. This was to teach and strengthen the church. Saul (Paul) and Barnabas were eventually sent out from Antioch to embark on more missionary journeys.

Sometimes we only have a small window of opportunity to pursue a particular purpose. God may place something on our heart that is only meant to be for a time and season. When we went out as missionaries we knew that it would only be for a time and a season. We thought we would be away for one year and ended up staying six years. After one year we were thinking of returning to Australia, but we had a guest speaker from England, who had a prophecy over us saying even though the College was functional, it was not established in the realm of the Spirit. He said it would take at least another two years for this to happen. He was right, it took another two years to establish it in the realm of the Spirit before we handed it over to the nationals to lead.

## A time and a season for everything

We often see that Churches will run a particular programme for a time and season. For example things like the 'Alpha' programme or the 'Careforce Lifekeys' series and so on.

> *'To everything, there is a **season**, a time for every **purpose** under heaven.'*
>
> Ecclesiastes 3:1

Our calling and ministry may remain the same with some slight adjustments. But our involvement in different things may only be for a time and season.

## The leading of the Holy Spirit

Paul was often led by the Holy Spirit to pursue a particular purpose for a given time and place. We read that he was planning his journey according to the leading of the Spirit.

> *'When these things were accomplished, Paul purposed in the **Spirit**, when he had passed through Macedonia and Achaia, to go to Jerusalem, saying "After I have been there, I must also see Rome".*
>
> Acts 19:21

We can easily miss a time and a season in God if we ignore the prompting of the Holy Spirit. We have to realise there are times and seasons in God for everything. May we choose wisely.

## Missed Opportunities

In retrospect, you may realize that you missed the leading and prompting of the Holy Spirit. You may have failed to obey God and take a step of faith, or you let the devil talk you out of it because of a fear of failure. It is important for you to seize the opportunity when you have it.

Today ministers often stay longer in one place. It is not an issue of how long you are in one place, but what you do with your time in that place. Hopefully, you will follow the leading of the Holy Spirit to know the right time and the season to pursue a particular purpose? I will list some of the things that have helped me to follow the leading of the Holy Spirit –

1. The inner witness of the Spirit.
2. When a door of opportunity opens.
3. Test the waters before leaping in. (a fleece)
4. Oversight Confirmation. (other leaders)
5. Stepping out in Faith. (go and do it)
6. Sensing when to bring things to a closure.
7. Knowing when to move on. (another season)

This list is by no means foolproof. They are some things that have helped me over the years to sense the right time and season to pursue whatever possibilities have been set before me.

## In the wrong place at the wrong time

We can be in the wrong place at the wrong time. This can be disastrous. This is the reason King David had an adulterous affair with Bathsheba.

> '...At a **time when King's go out to battle**...*that it happened one evening that David arose from his bed and walked on the roof of the King's house. And from the roof, he saw a woman bathing, and the woman was very beautiful to behold'.*
>
> 2 Samuel 11:1-2

King David was in the wrong place at the wrong time. He should have been on the battlefield. Instead, he became infatuated with Bathsheba. So he began to pursue a course of action that was disastrous for him.

I once had a minister tell me that he was going to a particular city whether God was in it or not. Things went okay for a short time and then disaster struck. It is too embarrassing to reveal what happened, but it was a terrible time for him and his family. However by the grace of God they relocated and continued to minister.

## Discerning the times

We need discernment to discern the times and the

seasons. We need to be observant and sensitive to certain signs that indicate the spiritual climate in our church and in our lives. Jesus said;

*'Discern the signs of the times'.*

Matthew 16:3

## What about times of unanswered prayer?

This is a difficult question to answer. One we all grapple with. In fact, I do not think there is a satisfactory answer. Over the years I have been healed, I have prayed and seen others healed. So it always puzzles me when nothing happens.

When we were in Lismore the whole church prayed and fasted for a man in our church that was dying of Leukemia. We all expected him to be healed. However, at 49 years of age, he went home to be with the Lord, leaving behind his wife and three young daughters. As a church, we were devastated. It was a really difficult time and season.

Most of us would probably have similar stories of times of unanswered prayer.

Our youngest daughter Sharon and her husband Jeremie have four lovely children, but they have been through the heartache of ten miscarriages in the process. Each time believing for a baby. You have to admire their courage and persistence.

I have enjoyed good health, but have had to have several Skin Cancers surgically removed. Every time I had a biopsy I had been believing for a better result. Recently I had to have prostate surgery which was completely unexpected as I was again believing for healing. Even though I thank God for modern medicine, I know God is well able to heal, but when it doesn't happen the way we thought it would it can be a tough time and season for us.

## A purpose that never changes

There is a purpose however that does not change. Despite the times and the seasons, there is one purpose that remains constant. It is the great commission of Christ. To go into all the world to proclaim the gospel.

Paul writes to young Timothy and encourages him to be ready to preach the word in season or out of season.

*'Preach the word! Be ready **in season** and **out of season**'.*

2 Timothy 4:2

I love the way the Amplified Bible expounds this

*'Herald and preach the word! Keep your sense of urgency (standby be at hand and ready, whether the opportunity seems to be **favorable or unfavorable**, whether it is **convenient or inconvenient**. Whether it be **welcome or unwelcome**...'*

So this scripture tells us that we should be ready to proclaim the gospel at all times regardless of circumstances. It is always the right time and season to proclaim the gospel.

# Chapter 16
## Pressing on with Purpose

We need to press on and pursue whatever it is that God is calling us to do. What has God set before you? The believers at Antioch were encouraged to continue with the Lord. They were to be continually pressing on regardless of any opposition that they may have been facing.

Christianity is a work in progress. We need to learn to grow in the knowledge of Christ. Spiritually we start off as newborn babes and hopefully grow into mature adults. Over the years I have seen many people turn to the Lord. Lives have been dramatically changed. Many start off spiritually as infants, then they grow and mature, with some ending up in the ministry.

I have been involved in outpourings of the Holy Spirit. Seen people baptized in water and in the power of the Holy Spirit. I have seen healings and miracles. I have been involved in the training of young men and women releasing them to find their place in ministry. But I firmly believe the best is yet to come.

The best outpourings of the Holy Spirit. The best Conversions. The best Healings and Miracles. The best Leaders and the best Churches are yet to come.

> '... *The Glory of this latter temple shall be* **greater than the former**, *says the Lord of Hosts'.*
>
> Haggai 2:9

## Unlimited potential in these last days

We truly live in a day of unlimited potential. With the advantage of modern technology, the power of a purpose-driven people today is unlimited.

> '...*now nothing they* **purpose** *to do will be withheld from them'.*
>
> Genesis 11:6

Although this is in the context of the building of the tower of Babel and God was not happy with their pride at that time. They were meant to scatter all over the world. They just wanted to stay in one place. However, it still reveals to us that people with a purpose have unlimited potential. But it needs to be a God-given purpose.

Today, the spread of the gospel can be at a rapid rate. In the beginning, Adam and Eve were to fill the earth and subdue it. This, of course, would not have been possible in their time. But today anything and everything is possible with the advanced technology we have at our disposal.

*'Be fruitful and multiply;* ***fill the earth and subdue it'.***

Genesis 1:28

For example, in Australia, we see the rise of Mega Churches like 'Hillsong', who are rapidly spreading the gospel in Australia and overseas.

## Reaching forward to things ahead

I have heard some ministers continually talk about the 'Good Old Days'. They have had some interesting things to say. But they are always looking back rather than looking forward. Paul says;

*'...I press on... forgetting those things which are behind. And* ***reaching forward*** *to those things which are ahead'.*

Philippians 3:12-13

Reflection is good, but we need to learn what we can from it. Then press on to embrace what God is wanting to do now and in the future. To do this we would be wise to be updating our vision and goals on a regular basis. This should inspire us to press on. What is the Holy Spirit saying to the church today?

*'He that has an ear, let him* ***hear*** *what the Spirit says to the Churches'.*

Revelation 2:7

## Fasting and Prayer

To hear from the Holy Spirit we may at times need to fast and pray. When we were about to return to Australia I decided to seek the Lord and fasted and prayed for direction. I would drive up into the hills every afternoon after lectures and walk around the bush praying. I only intended doing this for about a week and ended up going for much longer. I kept a journal and still look at and use some of the notes I made. I believe my prayers were answered as not long after I received an invitation to take over a church back in Australia.

## A heart for future generations

We are not going to be around forever. The day will come when we need to pass on the baton of faith to the next generation. If we are in leadership we should be preparing a successor to take over when the time is right. David expressed it this way -

> *'...when I am old and grey-headed, O God do not forsake me, until I declare your strength to* **this generation**, *your power to* ***everyone who is to come***'.
>
> Psalm 71:18

David wanted to pass on the baton to future generations. David also wanted to build a temple for God. But his son Solomon completed this task. His dream became his son's destiny. Solomon said;

*'I propose to build a house for the name of the Lord my God, as the Lord spoke to my Father...'*

1 Kings 5:5

Your dream may become someone else's destiny.

## The danger of complacency

Some ministers are too complacent. They become so Self Centred they do not care about handing on the baton. When Isaiah the prophet told King Hezekiah that his descendants would become eunuchs and taken captive. His reaction was like 'who cares', he said "as long as I have peace in my days" (2 Kings 20:19). He became complacent and showed no compassion or interest in future generations.

## Open to Times of Refreshing and New Things

I would like to think that the Church would be open to both times of refreshing and new things if we are going to press on into the future.

Firstly, Times of refreshing usually come from the presence of the Lord. This is often a result of people seeking the Lord. Soaking in His presence. Repenting of any sins that may be hindering their relationship with the Lord. Allowing the grace of God to bring healing into their lives.

*'...so that **times of refreshing** may come from the **presence** of the Lord'.*

Acts 3:19

This is often accompanied by fresh waves of the Holy Spirit. Apart from the basic doctrines we preach and teach. I have seen waves of the gifts of the Holy Spirit with an emphasis on some more than others. For example some outstanding Words of Knowledge. Other moves I have witnessed like – The Dancing move, The Leg Growing move. I saw a man with a built-up boot have his leg grow almost 2 inches. He went around with his boot giving his testimony. The Discipleship move. The Laughing move. The Seeker Friendly move, The Worship and Soaking in the Presence move and so on. These moves can be repetitive and seem to come in cycles. They are much needed times of refreshing.

Secondly, we need to be open to New Things. Perhaps a fresh new wave of the Spirit. Something we have not yet experienced.

*'Behold I will do a **New thing**…'*

Isaiah 43:19

We need to be thinking like the apostle Paul who spread the gospel 'Not just with persuasive words of human wisdom, but in demonstration of the Spirit and of power, that your faith should not be in the wisdom of men but in the power of God'. (1 Corinthians 2:4). We live in an educated world that values respectability and tradition, but we need to be constantly aware of the power of the Holy Spirit as we press on into the future. This is a New Day and we need to be hearing from the Lord and be willing to obey.

*'Today if you will* **hear His voice**,
*do not harden your hearts'.*

Hebrews 4:7

## Awakening Australia

In November 2018 we witnessed one of the greatest moves of God we have seen for some time in Australia. It was called 'Awakening Australia', held at 'Marvel Stadium' in Melbourne. An estimated 15,000 Christians gathered each day from different denominations. They came from all over Australia, to worship, and hear a number of great speakers. Many of these Christians went out and witnessed in the streets. They invited people back, many were saved, healed and delivered in the meetings. This was followed by baptisms at St.Kilda Beach.

## Developing a greater hunger for God

When I was first saved I had a tremendous hunger for God. I would devour the latest Christian Books and tapes, reading and listening and studying with my bible. I never missed the opportunity to fellowship with other like-minded Christians. That hunger has never really left me. It is something we need to foster more and more in ourselves and others today as we press on. Jesus said;

*'Blessed are those who* **hunger and thirst** *for righteousness for they shall be filled'*

Matthew 5:6

## Exciting days ahead of us

We are living in exciting days. We have a great future ahead of us. May we rise to the challenge of presenting the gospel in our community. We have great opportunities to spread the gospel with our modern technology and creative abilities today. We will have had our disappointments and setbacks but we still need to keep pressing on.

We need to be full of expectation for the future, just like the people were in expectation of a coming Messiah in the days of John the Baptist and Jesus.

> '...*the people were in **expectation**, and all reasoned in their hearts about John, whether he was the Christ or not'.*
>
> Luke 3:15

I expect that the best is yet to come. I hope that you too will live in expectation of a greater future for yourself. Be open to the leading and prompting of the Holy Spirit as to where you fit in. Press on into whatever that may be.

I pray that having read this book, it will have helped you to unlock and discover your God-given purpose in life and that you will pursue it with a passion.

www.ingramcontent.com/pod-product-compliance
Lightning Source LLC
Chambersburg PA
CBHW031422290426
44110CB00011B/484